THE OFFICIAL

BRIDGERTON
COOKBOOK

THE OFFICIAL
BRIDGERTON
COOKBOOK

REGULA YSEWIJN
With RECIPES *by* SUSAN VU

shondaland | NETFLIX

RANDOM HOUSE WORLDS
NEW YORK

CONTENTS

Lady Whistledown's
SOCIETY PAPERS

EXTRAORDINARY PEOPLE. EXTRAORDINARY NEWS

Dearest Gentle Reader,

At long last, London's smart set has made its return after a lazy, and dare I say dull, off-season sojourn in the country. As a new season presents itself, the ton yearns for something fresh, exciting, and—this author hopes—deliciously newsworthy to entertain and enthrall. With at least two balls to attend each week, and social obligations that include opera engagements, the theatre, promenading, and entertaining morning callers and potential suitors, the season is not all feathers, frivolity, and Champagne glasses; it's work! So sharpen your wit, your wardrobe, and your knives, dear reader, and wield this cookery book to your advantage as you prepare to fuel and charm with scintillating savories and seductive sweets.

This author shall sharpen her quill in anticipation of many kitchen scandals to come.

Yours truly,

Lady Whistledown

INTRODUCTION

Bridgerton, our most beloved embodiment of Regency Britain, unfurls before us like a rich and vibrant tapestry, where every thread shimmers with life and excitement—from the opulent settings and the lavish gowns to the captivating characters and the sumptuous dishes that grace their tables. Here is the dazzling world of the ton, a society within a society comprising high-ranking members of the peerage and their immediate (and often, meddlesome) relations, as well as those seeking entrance to this gilded community by way of wit, work, or wont of a good marriage.

To survive and thrive at this upper echelon of society requires a combination of good breeding, impeccable manners, fine taste, and of course, a reputation that is beyond reproach. It also demands a miscellany of talents. To successfully navigate the annual social season, a time when the well-regarded families of the ton open their homes for lavish receptions and balls, one must be a witty conversationalist, an accomplished musician and dancer, a careful student of society's rules and etiquette, and perhaps most important, a flawless host and guest. Obstinate fathers, ambitious mamas, social-climbing suitors, and jealous competitors will conspire to ruin a family's carefully curated reputation, but these obstacles must be overcome.

Be it grand events such as Lady Danbury's first ball of the season or Her Majesty the Queen's exquisite annual luncheon, or more select soirées such as those for the married ladies of the ton or debaucherous gatherings for freethinking artists, there are endless opportunities to see and be seen, to impress and be impressed throughout the season. In the same way the ton eagerly await the crowning of the Diamond of the Season, one ardently anticipates which grand affair shall be considered the incomparable *event* of the season. Which dinner party or ball shall set the stage for the most desirable matches, the most spirited quadrilles, the most delightful dinner party anecdotes, the most interesting menus, and the most scandalous morning-after gossip on the promenade? One salivates in expectation . . .

AN AGE OF APPETITES

Bridgerton's Regency era is named for a period in the early 1800s when George IV served as Prince Regent (ruler) while his father, King George III, was incapacitated. This was a time known for its elegance, refinement, and extravagant parties. Lavish soirées and glittering balls held in grand mansions and elegant ballrooms were the order of the day. No expense was spared as families such as the Bridgertons, the Featheringtons, and the Cowpers engaged in a relentless pursuit of entertainment. The social calendar was meticulously planned, and its events were carefully dressed for and diligently attended.

In Bridgerton, the social season, when society's highest return to London from their country estates, is when the ton get busy with the serious business of socializing. The season is not only an opportunity for the aristocracy to showcase their wealth, social standing, and fashion-forward taste, but also an important arena for courtships and strategic alliances, and a chance to rub shoulders with barons, dukes, and princes in the pursuit of social prominence. Feasts are dominated by monumental displays of seafood, game birds, and meat. Plates of food are carefully arranged on a pristine white tablecloth and, when possible, presented with a touch of theatrical flair.

For marriage-minded mamas laser-focused on finding a good match for their eligible offspring, the presentation of debutantes to the Queen at court sets the tone for the season. This event showcases the available offspring of the ton's finest families and serves as an announcement that families are open to proposals of marriage. If a young lady is fortunate enough to capture the Queen's attention with her beauty and poise, as Daphne Bridgerton and Edwina Sharma did in recent years, she might be bestowed the highest honor of being declared the incomparable Diamond of the First Water. This blessing all but guarantees a fortuitous match and a season filled with potential suitors competing for her attention, for a place on her dance card, and for her hand.

ENTERTAINING THE TON

Whether you are hosting a gathering of the married ladies of the ton so that they may network; taking afternoon tea with the mother of a potential suitor while your lady's maid gets the scoop from your guest's maid; or you are simply hoping to fan the flames of affection between a diamond and a duke, you must always strive for perfection in your presentation. Elaborate affairs such as Lady Danbury's first ball of the season and Daphne and Simon's grand Hastings Ball require an army of behind-the-scenes staff, but there are lessons to be gleaned for even the least experienced of hosts.

ELABORATE CENTERPIECES

Less is never more when it comes to entertaining the ton. To add to the drama of a dinner or, perhaps, to *create* drama for courting lovers attempting to make eye contact across a table, the finer homes will typically commission a sugar as a centerpiece. These are generally fantastical and fanciful, and intended to be admired, not eaten— an extravagant display for the host to flaunt. Mere mortals might consider a tower of cream puffs bound together with caramel, a croquembouche (see page 236), as a centerpiece that is impressive but also edible.

SET THE SCENE

While the best-laid plans often go awry, the best-laid tables are an entirely different matter. Whether it is afternoon tea with a bestie, or a boisterous soirée to test the talents of the ton's suitors, one must create the perfect setting if one wants drama. And one wants drama! The table must be set with the crispest of white linens, upon which the family silver, one's best china, delicate candlesticks, and elaborate floral displays are placed. If you don't have your own engraved silver or a full set of Wedgwood dishes (yet . . . the season is young!), one can visit estate sales, thrift stores, and yard sales to find affordable ornate pieces to inspire fancy. Remember, more is more, so snap up mismatched china, etched glasses and vases, and antique silver pieces.

If creativity is the focus for the table setting, then strategy is the name of the game when it comes to seating. Just as a dance is choreographed movement, one must take the utmost care in ensuring vulgar mamas and social-climbing suitors are not within gloved elbow reach of your more esteemed guests. If you have a Cressida

Cowper in your social circle, you will want to watch your eligible bachelors (and your solo strolls in the garden), and if you are fortunate enough to be blessed with the presence of a baron or duke, you will want to ensure they have a prime seat at your side.

CONSIDER YOUR GUESTS

While candles and towers of candies are sure to excite and delight your guests, a true host knows it is the smaller, more discreet moves that truly enchant. Take Lady Bridgerton's thoughtful and strategic inclusion of gooseberry pie (see page 149), the Duke's favorite dessert, at dinner. Make a habit of noting what your guests enjoy and put it into your plan. Is there a favorite color? Perhaps make it a subtle theme of the evening. A preferred composer? Instruct your orchestra (or playlist) to make it the evening's soundtrack. Did your guest comment on how great your True Love Biscuits (page 74) was last time? Create a pretty little takeaway package for their carriage ride home. It may seem that Lady Whistledown is the only one paying attention at these events, but a few thoughtful notes when entertaining will show you that we all warm to a little attention.

LEAVE THEM WANTING MORE

While you will no doubt win new hearts and fans with your rendition of Lady Edwina's India Pepper Pot (page 177) and find that an invitation to your table will be most coveted once you produce your large free-standing pie of game and fowl (see page 129) you will always want to send your guests away with a favorable last impression—that of your dessert skills. Dinner in the season can leave little room for dessert, so you may limit your menu to three or four courses and ensure your last course is a collection of precious jewels, with Pâte de Fruits (page 105), comfits, and other confectionery arranged like gemstones in a jewelry box. Creams like the pistachio cream Brimsley and Reynolds share (see page 241), jellies like the Jaune Mange (page 227), and

Yorkshire Puddings (page 34) should be served on delicate dessert plates or artfully presented on tiered trays.

A TRUE BRIDGERTON COOKBOOK

Who doesn't want to spend more time in the world of Bridgerton? This cookbook opens up this delightful world and invites us to eat and drink like our favorite families. While many of these recipes have roots in the Regency era, we've taken a cue from Bridgerton and infused more color and, yes, convenience into these seventy recipes. In Bridgerton's world, the Empire waist might dominate, but the historically accurate bonnets of the time are conspicuously absent. Do we care? Not at all. Colorful macaron towers may be a significant fixture on festive Bridgerton tables, but these delicate delights, including our more generously sized Pink Perfections (see page 233), made their debut only in the early twentieth century. Likewise, the pristine, four-foot-tall white wedding cake, complete with the Bridgerton and Hastings crest, looks perfectly at home at Daphne and Simon's nuptials, yet this kind of cake was absent in the actual Regency period. (Baking powder, which bestows a lightness to our creation, had yet to be discovered.) The pursuit of absolute historical authenticity might find us simmering calf's feet for hours to craft the essential gelatin for those famed Regency jellies (see page 80), which were indeed a massive Regency dinner trend among the elite. Instead, we offer you the modern convenience of gelatin powder. You're welcome.

The
BRIDGERTONS

*"I realize it may be unfashionable,
but we rather like each other."*
—VIOLET BRIDGERTON

The Bridgerton family comprises the matriarch, Lady
Violet, and her lively group of eight children, all bearing
alphabetical names: Anthony, Benedict, Colin, Daphne,
Eloise, Francesca, Gregory, and Hyacinth. Despite the
tragic loss of their father, the Bridgertons have stuck
together and their household radiates warmth, humor, and
intelligence. Violet allows all eight children to sit at the
adult table, transcending the typical decorum of Regency-
era dinner gatherings. This inclusivity results in a rapid
crossfire of conversation from all ages (and the occasional
throwing of peas). For guests like the Duke of Hastings,
who grew up in a lonely, formal house, the Bridgerton
dinner table is both unconventional and charming.

Lady Violet works with her kitchen staff to create
traditional but delicious meals that appeal to all ages
and can be served family style, so eight hungry children
have a chance of getting first dibs of their favorite food.
The youngest Bridgertons enjoy the Succulent Stuffed
Lettuce and the Tattie Scones. Eloise likes the simplicity
of a Victoria Sandwich Cake because she shies away from
anything too frivolous. We can see the influence of Colin's
European travels with the Greek-inspired fish dish Whole
Lavraki and the Aegean Fasolada, a flavorsome bean soup.
Benedict is not forgotten; he would be happy to snatch
a Perfect Pork Pie from the kitchen late in the evening,
when coming home from the artist studio and feeling
peckish. There is something for all the Bridgertons in this
chapter, for it is food that keeps a household happy.

TATTIE SCONES

Served with eggs and smoked salmon or kippers, along with a side salad, these flat Scottish potato cakes are perfect for a hearty Bridgerton breakfast. Tattie Scones also make an ideal late-night snack for Benedict Bridgerton, who as an artist usually spends long days in the studio. The ever-prepared Bridgerton cook keeps any leftovers from breakfast just for this purpose to easily reheat in a hot pan.

Makes 16 scones

1 cup all-purpose flour, plus additional for dusting	1 pound russet potatoes (about 2 large)	3 tablespoons unsalted butter, at room temperature
1 teaspoon baking powder	Kosher salt	Freshly ground black pepper

COOK'S NOTE: *You can make a sweet potato version of these scones by replacing the russet potatoes with orange-hued sweet potatoes, but you will need an additional ¼ to ⅓ cup of flour for the dough because sweet potatoes tend to be more moist than white baking potatoes.*

1. In a medium bowl, whisk together the flour and baking powder. Line a large baking sheet with parchment and dust with a light coating of flour.

2. Put the potatoes into a large saucepan and cover with enough water to cover by 1 inch. Bring to a boil over medium-high heat, about 15 minutes. Stir in a generous amount of salt and cook until the potatoes are fork-tender, about 20 additional minutes. Drain and set the potatoes aside to cool slightly, about 10 minutes.

3. Once cool enough to handle, peel the potatoes and place into a medium bowl. Add the butter, 1 teaspoon salt, and several large grinds of pepper, then mash well until mostly smooth (a few small lumps are fine). Add the flour mixture and mix with a rubber spatula or wooden spoon until mostly combined.

4. Use your hands to bring the dough together until it is smooth and supple. Lightly dust your work surface with flour, and turn out the dough onto the counter. Dust your hands with more flour, then form the dough into a disk about 1 inch thick. Cut the disk into 4 equal portions.

5. Working with one portion of dough at a time (cover the remaining dough with a kitchen towel), roll the dough into a 6-inch round that is about ¼ inch thick. Quarter

recipe continues

the round to create 4 wedges. then transfer the wedges to the baking sheet. Repeat with the remaining dough disks to make 16 scones.

6. Warm a large cast-iron skillet on medium to medium-high heat. When hot, use a wide flat metal spatula to lay 4 to 6 scones in the hot, dry skillet. Cook until browned and crispy on the first side, 3 to 5 minutes. Carefully turn the scones over and cook until the second side is also browned and crispy, 3 to 5 additional minutes. Transfer to a large platter, overlapping if necessary, and cover loosely with foil or a kitchen towel to keep warm while you cook the remaining scones.

7. Serve the warm Tattie Scones with your favorite style of eggs (fried, or a soft scramble is particularly delicious) or serve as part of a large breakfast grazing board with your favorite fresh and/or pickled vegetables, fruit, smoked fish, griddled sausages, and the like.

AEGEAN FASOLADA

"If you loved it there [Greece] so much, why did you ever return home?"
—ELOISE

Fasolada is a white bean soup Colin enjoyed during his travels to Greece, bringing to mind the bean dishes that had been a comforting nursery delight for him. This particular recipe transforms into a more elegant soup fit for a Bridgerton meal. The secret of this dish is a hint of oregano, complemented by a drizzle of olive oil just before serving. Rich in fiber, protein, iron, and vitamin B, this bean soup is a great brunch, lunch, dinner, or even a delightful late-night repast when paired with a few slices of perfectly toasted bread.

Makes 6 to 8 servings

12 ounces dried small white beans, such as navy or cannellini (about 1¼ cups)

Kosher salt

6 tablespoons extra-virgin olive oil, plus additional for drizzling

1 large yellow onion, coarsely chopped

3 medium carrots, peeled and coarsely chopped

3 celery stalks, trimmed and coarsely chopped

4 garlic cloves, minced

3 tablespoons tomato paste

2 large semi-waxy potatoes, such as Yukon Gold, cut into roughly ½-inch pieces

Pinch of red pepper flakes, plus additional for serving

1½ teaspoons dried oregano

2 dried bay leaves

8 cups water

Toasted bread, for serving

1. Place the beans in a medium bowl, then add enough water to cover by 2 inches. Season with a large pinch of salt, give the beans a stir, then refrigerate and soak the beans at least 8 hours and up to overnight.

2. Drain the beans and rinse well. Put them in a large saucepan and cover with at least 2 inches of water. Bring to a boil over medium-high heat, then reduce the heat to medium-low and simmer until the beans are just barely tender (taste a couple of beans; they should not be hard, but they should still have a bite), stirring occasionally and spooning off any foam that rises to the top, 10 to 15 minutes. Drain the beans, transfer to a medium bowl, and cover with a damp paper towel.

recipe continues

3. In a large Dutch oven or other heavy-bottomed pot over medium heat, warm 3 tablespoons of the olive oil, then add the onion, carrots, and celery. Season with salt and cook, stirring occasionally, until the vegetables start to be tender, about 10 minutes. Add the garlic and cook, stirring constantly, until softened, about 2 minutes. Increase the heat slightly and add the tomato paste and cook, stirring constantly, for 2 minutes. Add the drained beans, then add the potatoes, red pepper flakes, oregano, and bay leaf, and stir to combine. Pour in the water and bring to a boil, then cook for about 20 minutes, stirring occasionally. Reduce the heat to low, cover partially with the lid, and let the soup simmer, skimming the top and giving everything a good stir occasionally, until the beans are very tender (almost creamy) and the broth is slightly thickened, about 1 ½ hours. (If needed, add more water during the cooking process so the beans and vegetables are always covered.)

4. Stir in the remaining 3 tablespoons olive oil and season the finished soup with a good amount of salt. Simmer the soup over low heat until the broth is rich and velvety, about 10 additional minutes. Discard the bay leaves and ladle the hot soup into serving bowls. Top each serving with a good drizzle of additional olive oil. Serve immediately, with good crusty, toasted bread and a small bowl of red pepper flakes on the side.

PERFECT PORK PIE

❧

Pork pies have a long tradition in Britain. They come in all sizes, from snuff-box size to huge wheels meant to serve a party of twenty, but the most popular were those made in a pocket size. Pork pies are always made with hot water–crust pastry, which is one of the easiest and most satisfying pastries to make. The meat inside is compact, which makes it simple to cut the pies into neat wedges—easily snatched from the kitchen by one of the Bridgerton boys, then wrapped in a pristine white napkin and eaten while rushing to somewhere fun. For the Bridgertons, these pies are a favorite for luncheons and garden picnics, great on their own, or served with a green salad and topped with a dollop of strong mustard.

Serves 6

FOR THE HOT WATER CRUST

3 cups all-purpose flour, sifted, plus more for dusting

1½ cups bread flour, sifted

1¼ cups water

¾ cup pork lard, at room temperature

Kosher salt

1 large egg, lightly beaten

FOR THE PORK FILLING

1 small leek

1 pound boneless pork shoulder, cut into roughly ¼-inch pieces

6 ounces thick-cut bacon, cut into roughly ¼-inch pieces

1 teaspoon freshly grated nutmeg

¼ teaspoon mace

Kosher salt and freshly ground black pepper

FOR THE SALAD

1 teaspoon white wine vinegar

½ teaspoon Dijon mustard, plus extra for serving

Kosher salt and freshly ground black pepper

¼ cup extra-virgin olive oil

3 cups tender greens, such as frisée, arugula, watercress, and/or microgreens

SPECIAL EQUIPMENT:
1 (7-inch) round biscuit cutter and 1 (4-inch) round biscuit cutter

COOK'S NOTE: *To make cutting the pork shoulder and bacon easier, chill the meat in advance. Do not be tempted to use a food processor, since that will give the filling a gummy texture.*

This dough is flexible and easy to work with. If there are any tears or holes as you are forming the pork pies, just use a bit of excess dough to patch them. You can also refrigerate the dough until it is chilled again if it becomes too soft to handle easily.

The pork pies can be assembled, brushed with egg wash, then refrigerated for several hours before baking.

recipe continues

1. MAKE THE CRUST: In a large bowl, whisk together the 3 cups all-purpose flour and the bread flour.

2. In a medium saucepan over medium heat, combine the water, lard, and 1 teaspoon salt. Bring the mixture to a simmer and stir until the lard melts and everything is evenly combined, 6 to 8 minutes. Pour the simmering water-and-lard mixture into the bowl of flour and use a wooden spoon to stir the ingredients until a crumbly and shaggy dough forms.

3. Turn the dough out onto a piece of parchment and use your hands to knead the dough until it holds together and is somewhat smooth, about 1 minute. (Do not add any flour to the parchment to knead the dough.) Shape the dough into a rectangle about ¾ inch thick; this will make dividing it easier later. Wrap in parchment and refrigerate the dough until completely chilled, about 3 hours.

4. MAKE THE FILLING: Trim off the root end and cut away the tough dark green top from the leek, then cut the leek lengthwise in half and then cut the halves in half again. Thinly slice each leek quarter crosswise into ⅛-inch pieces (about 1 cup). Transfer the leek slices to a medium bowl. Fill the bowl with cold water and use your hands to separate the pieces and coax out any dirt. Drain through a fine-mesh strainer and repeat this process until there is no dirt left on the leek. Dry the leek pieces well.

5. Put the chopped pork in a large bowl.

6. In a large skillet, combine the bacon, the leek pieces, the nutmeg, mace, 1½ teaspoons salt, and ¼ teaspoon pepper. Place the skillet over medium heat and cook, stirring occasionally, until the fat starts to render from the bacon, about 5 minutes. Continue to cook, stirring occasionally, until the leek is soft and the bacon is fully cooked but not yet crisp, 6 to 8 additional minutes.

7. Add the sautéed ingredients to the bowl with the pork, making sure to scrape all the rendered fat into the bowl as well. Let cool enough to handle (5 to 10 minutes), then use your hands to mix the ingredients until the leek and bacon are evenly distributed through the pork. Refrigerate until ready to use.

8. ASSEMBLE AND BAKE THE PIES: Line 2 baking sheets with parchment.

9. Remove the chilled dough from the refrigerator. Lightly dust your work surface and a rolling pin with flour. Cut the dough into 3 equal pieces. Working with one piece at a time, roll the dough into a large round ¼ inch thick, rotating the dough as needed so it doesn't stick. Use a 7-inch round biscuit cutter and a 4-inch round biscuit cutter to cut out 2 large rounds and 2 smaller rounds from the dough, rerolling the scraps if needed to get 4 rounds. (Alternatively, use 2 bowls that match these widths and a paring knife to cut out the rounds.) Set the rounds on one of the baking sheets. Repeat rolling and cutting out the rounds with the remaining dough so you have 6 large rounds and 6 small rounds. Refrigerate the small rounds.

10. Preheat the oven to 350°F.

11. Choose a jar or glass that has approximately a 3-inch base. Lightly dust the outside of the jar with flour. Gently place the jar in the center of one of the large dough rounds. Use your hands to gently press the dough up around the side of the jar. Flip the jar over, so now the dough is on top; this will make it easier to fill. Continue to smooth the dough against the side of the jar. The side of the dough should be about 2 inches high all around. (You shouldn't need to stretch the dough to get that size; simply help it take the shape of the jar by pressing and smoothing the sides.) With one hand on the dough and one hand on the jar, gently wiggle the jar out of the dough, then place the dough cup on the baking sheet, open side up, and refrigerate. Repeat with the remaining 5 large rounds.

12. Remove the filling, the dough cups, and the smaller dough rounds from the refrigerator. Divide the filling evenly among the 6 cups, putting approximately ½ cup filling in each cup. Brush the exposed dough inside each cup with some of the beaten egg. Place the smaller dough rounds on top, gently pushing the centers down so they meet and completely cover the filling. Using your thumb and index finger, press the lids and sides of the cups together, brushing with more beaten egg, if needed, to help adhere the dough. As you press the 2 doughs together, you will form a ½-inch rim. Use a paring knife to make a small slit in the top of each lid to create a vent.

13. Place the 6 assembled pies back on one of the baking sheets and brush the sides and tops of them with more beaten egg. Bake until the pies are golden brown all over and the dough is cooked through, about 1 hour, rotating the baking sheet once after 30 minutes. Remove from the oven and let the pork pies cool slightly while you make the salad.

14. MAKE THE SALAD AND SERVE: In a medium bowl, whisk together the vinegar, ½ teaspoon mustard, and a pinch of salt and pepper. Slowly stream in the olive oil, whisking constantly, until the dressing is emulsified. Add the tender greens to the bowl and toss to coat with the dressing.

15. Place the pork pies on 6 individual plates. Divide the salad among the plates and serve immediately, with a side of additional mustard.

BRIDGERTON SUNDAY ROAST
with Burnt Onion Gravy

———————◆———————

These days, a typical Sunday roast is something the British enjoy eating out, preferably in a village pub with a roaring fire. In the Regency era, it was very much a meal at the heart of the family home, and is especially so at the Bridgerton house. The well-connected Bridgerton kitchen staff has first dibs at the butcher's shop for choosing the best pieces of meat. Several essential components must accompany the chosen roasted meat to achieve the epitome of an English Sunday roast: crispy roast potatoes, affectionately referred to as "roasties," which provide a satisfying crunch and have the youngest Bridgertons fighting for the last morsel; parsnips and/or carrots, delicately glazed with thyme and honey for a touch of sweetness; a luscious burnt onion gravy; and of course, Yorkshire puddings, from a light baked batter that's designed to absorb and savor every drop of gravy.

Makes 6 servings

1 (5- to 6-pound) bone-in beef rib roast

Kosher salt and freshly ground black pepper

12 large sprigs of fresh rosemary

2½ pounds fingerling potatoes

2 tablespoons plus 2 teaspoons vegetable oil

1 medium yellow onion, thickly sliced

3 tablespoons extra-virgin olive oil

1 pound parsnips, peeled and sliced diagonally ¼ inch thick

1 pound carrots, peeled and sliced diagonally ¼ inch thick

1½ teaspoons coarsely chopped fresh thyme

2 tablespoons unsalted butter

2 teaspoons honey

½ cup (4 ounces) dry red wine

¼ cup all-purpose flour

3½ cups beef stock

Yorkshire Puddings, for serving (page 34)

COOK'S NOTE: *A good gravy is the backbone of any roast dinner. Any leftover gravy here can be frozen to create a base for wonderful meals to come, a luxury Regency cooks did not have.*

1. Place the rib roast on a small baking sheet or large plate and season liberally all over with salt and pepper. Chill, uncovered, in the refrigerator for at least 2 hours and up to 48 hours.

2. Remove the rib roast from the refrigerator and let sit at room temperature for 30 minutes.

3. Meanwhile, fill a large pot with water and bring to a boil over high heat. Add 4 of the rosemary sprigs and season the water liberally with salt. Add the potatoes and

recipe continues

————————❋————————

cook until a fork inserted into a potato glides in but meets with some resistance (the potatoes should be only partially cooked at this point), 7 to 10 minutes. Drain.

4. Put one rack on the bottom shelf of the oven and place a baking sheet on the oven rack. Place a second rack on the shelf in the center of the oven and preheat the oven to 375°F.

5. In an extra-large cast-iron skillet over medium-high heat, warm 2 tablespoons of the vegetable oil until it starts to shimmer. Carefully lay the rib roast in the hot oil and sear the meat on all sides, rotating as needed so it browns evenly, about 15 minutes total. Transfer the roast to a plate.

6. Scatter the onion in the bottom of a large roasting pan, drizzle with the remaining 2 teaspoons vegetable oil, and season liberally with salt and pepper. Stir to combine and spread out in a single layer, then place a roasting rack on top of the onion. Briefly run the remaining 8 rosemary sprigs under cold water, flick them several times to get rid of excess water, then arrange on the rack. Place the seared beef on top of the rosemary.

7. Spoon out the beef fat from the skillet and reserve to make the Yorkshire Puddings; a little bit of fat left in the skillet is okay and there is no need to wash the skillet.

8. Roast the beef on the center rack until an instant-read thermometer inserted into the thickest part registers 125°F for medium-rare doneness, 1 hour 30 minutes to 2 hours 30 minutes (depending on the size of your roast). For medium doneness, instead roast the beef until it reaches 135°F, 30 to 60 additional minutes. The temperature of the roast will continue to rise after you take it out of the oven and let it rest.

9. After the beef has been in the oven for 1 hour, transfer the parcooked potatoes to a large bowl, drizzle with 2 tablespoons of the olive oil, season liberally with salt and pepper, then toss to coat. Scatter the potatoes on the preheated bottom baking

sheet and roast until browned in spots and fork-tender, 35 to
45 minutes, shaking the baking sheet several times while they
roast. Remove the potatoes from the oven and cover the hot
baking sheet loosely with foil to keep warm.

10. While the beef and potatoes are roasting, add the remaining
tablespoon olive oil to the cast-iron skillet and warm it on
medium to medium-high heat. When the oil is hot, add the
parsnips and carrots and season liberally with salt and pepper.
Cook, stirring occasionally, until the vegetables are browned in
spots and just starting to get tender, 8 to 10 minutes. Turn off
the heat, add the butter and the honey, and stir until the butter
is melted. Remove from the heat and let sit at room temperature
while the beef and potatoes cook.

11. Once the beef is cooked to your desired doneness, remove the
roasting pan from the oven and carefully transfer the roasting
rack with the rosemary and beef to a sheet pan or tray. Loosely
cover with foil and let rest while you finish the carrots and
parsnips, and make the gravy.

12. To the skillet with the carrots and parsnips, stir in the thyme, then transfer the
skillet to the center rack of the oven and roast until fork-tender, about 20 minutes.
Set a fine-mesh strainer over a medium bowl.

13. While the vegetables roast, spoon up any fat in the roasting pan that exceeds
3 tablespoons and save to make the Yorkshire Puddings.

14. Set the roasting pan over medium heat. (Depending on the size of your roasting
pan, you might have to set the pan over 2 burners.) Some of the onion might be
very charred, but that is okay and ideal for this particular gravy. When the fat
starts to bubble lightly, pour in the wine and cook until reduced by about half, 5 to
10 minutes, scraping up any browned bits at the bottom of the pan with a wooden
spoon. Sprinkle the flour over the onion and wine, then cook for 2 minutes, stirring
constantly. Gradually whisk in 3 cups of the stock until smooth (if there are a few
clumps of flour, it is okay, since you will be straining the finished gravy). Simmer the
gravy, whisking frequently, until thickened and deeply flavorful, 10 to 15 minutes. (If
the gravy is a touch too thick, whisk in a splash or two of the remaining stock until it
is your desired consistency.) Spoon the gravy into the strainer and discard the onion.
Season the gravy with salt and pepper, then transfer to a gravy boat.

15. To serve, cut the rib roast off the bone, then thinly slice the meat against the
grain and place the slices on a serving platter. Transfer the roasted potatoes and the
honey-glazed carrots and parsnips to serving bowls, and serve immediately alongside
the hot gravy and the freshly baked Yorkshire Puddings.

ROAST BEEF

Britain has been famous for its animal
husbandry and roasting skills since
the seventeenth century. The French
have called the British *"les rosbif"*
since 1774, precisely for that reason.
It would be expected by families of
the ton to present at least one
roasted meat dish to their guests. The
more offerings, the more you could
impress your guests. Both British
families today and those in the
Regency would often use several
types of meat. Venison and lamb are
acceptable, and small families often
choose a plump farmhouse chicken.
In the Georgian period, meat was
roasted in front of a roaring fire in a
large fireplace; luckily today we have
modern ovens that are up to the task
without causing smoke and requiring
lots of manual labor to turn the spit.

YORKSHIRE PUDDINGS

———————— ✦ ————————

Yorkshire pudding was known as a "dripping pudding" before it was given the name Yorkshire pudding. It was often eaten before the meat, with just gravy so as to suppress the appetite for the more expensive meat and thereby stretching it further. In the great family homes of the ton, however, one didn't need to be frugal and the Yorkshire puddings could be eaten with the meat.

The Bridgerton family cook usually prepares small individual Yorkshire puddings, but on occasions when the cook knows Anthony will be out riding his horses, the kitchen staff indulges him with a larger pudding that acts as a bowl on the dinner plate, allowing him to nestle the meat and vegetables within its embrace. So arranged, a pouring of the rich gravy envelopes the contents in savory delight.

Makes 12 servings

3 large eggs	2 tablespoons water	6 tablespoons rendered beef fat (from the Bridgerton Sunday Roast), beef tallow, duck fat, or bacon fat
1 large egg white	Kosher salt	
¾ cup whole milk	1 cup all-purpose flour, sifted	

1. Set a fine-mesh strainer over a 2-cup liquid measuring cup with a spout.

2. In a medium bowl, whisk together the eggs, egg white, milk, water, and 1 teaspoon salt until smooth. Add the flour and whisk vigorously until the batter is smooth. Pour through the strainer, then cover the measuring cup with plastic wrap and refrigerate for at least 1 hour and up to overnight.

3. Preheat the oven to 425°F.

4. Divide the rendered beef fat among the cups of a standard 12-cup muffin tin (1½ teaspoons per cup), then place the muffin tin on a baking sheet and put in the oven until very hot, about 10 minutes.

5. When the tin and beef fat are hot (the batter should sizzle when added to the oil), remove the batter from the refrigerator and give it a good stir. Have handy a paper towel or a kitchen towel. Remove the baking sheet from the oven and place on a trivet. Working quickly but carefully, fill each muffin cup halfway with the chilled batter, using the paper towel or kitchen towel to wipe the spout of the cup as needed so excess batter does not drip onto the muffin tin. (That extra batter will catch onto the Yorkshire puddings as they bake and drag them down, preventing your puddings

from rising properly.) If you have batter leftover after filling each cup halfway, evenly divide it among the 12 cups.

6. Return the muffin tin to the oven and bake until the puddings are puffed and almost tripled in size, golden brown, and crisp, about 20 minutes. (Note: The puddings will be lightly crisp with a custard center at this point, but they will most likely collapse shortly after being removed from the oven. For sturdier puddings that retain their shape, bake for 5 additional minutes, during which time the puddings will turn deep golden brown and get a tad drier (not as custardy in the center). Either version is delicious, but bake according to your preference. During the baking process, do not at any point open the oven door, but instead peek through the oven window to check on the puddings.

7. Remove the hot Yorkshire puddings from the muffin tin and serve immediately.

YORKSHIRE PUDDING

The first recipe for a Yorkshire pudding appeared in a 1747 cookbook by Hannah Glasse, called *The Art of Cookery Made Plain and Easy*. She instructs readers to "have a good piece of meat at the fire, take a stew-pan and put some dripping in, set it on the fire; when it boils, pour in your pudding; let it bake on the fire till you think it is nigh enough." Before there were ovens, meat was roasted on a spit, in front of the fire, and while the spit turned and the fat dripped down, that fat was collected in a dripping pan, which was then cleverly used for baking the pudding.

SUCCULENT STUFFED LETTUCE

Because all ages of Bridgertons gather around the table at mealtimes, Lady Violet Bridgerton insists on having the younger Bridgertons' favorite dishes set out among the more elegant dishes. This popular Georgian recipe has romaine lettuce stuffed with minced meat; it is so delicious that Francesca, Gregory, and Hyacinth often fight over the last one. Colin, having known this dish since childhood, was pleasantly surprised when he encountered these tasty meat parcels in Italy, where they are served with tomato sauce. The stuffed lettuce packages can be made a day in advance and can simply be heated in a microwave when you're ready to serve. Serve them with steamed vegetables and/or with mashed potatoes to soak up that wonderful sauce.

Makes 6 servings

FOR THE STUFFED LETTUCE

12 large romaine leaves
(the outer leaves from
2 or 3 large heads)

12 medium romaine leaves
(the slightly smaller leaves from
2 or 3 large heads)

1 small leek

¾ cup finely crumbled stale
white bread

1 large egg

2 tablespoons water

1 tablespoon vegetable oil

Kosher salt and freshly ground
black pepper

3 garlic cloves, minced

2 teaspoons finely chopped
fresh rosemary

1½ cups cooked wild rice

1½ pounds (93% lean) ground
turkey

½ teaspoon mace (optional)

16 long stems of fresh chives

½ cup turkey or chicken stock

2 tablespoons unsalted butter, cut
into 12 cubes, at room
temperature

FOR THE GRAVY

3 tablespoons unsalted butter

1 large shallot, finely diced

Kosher salt and freshly ground
black pepper

3 tablespoons all-purpose flour

2¼ cups turkey or chicken stock

1 teaspoon Worcestershire sauce

1. MAKE THE STUFFED LETTUCE: Lay a large romaine leaf on a cutting board and use a knife to cut away the thick stem that runs up the center of the lettuce, leaving as much of the leafy part as intact as possible. Repeat with the remaining 11 large leaves, stacking the leaves on a baking sheet as you trim them. Then, laying a

recipe continues

medium romaine leaf on the cutting board, cut away its thick stem and then cut the leaf in half to create 2 long strips. Repeat with the remaining 11 medium leaves, also stacking them on the baking sheet. (These strips will be used to patch the stuffed leaves as you form and roll them.)

2. Trim off the root and tough dark green top from the leek, then cut in half lengthwise and cut each half in half again to have 4 quarters. Thinly slice each leek quarter crosswise into ⅛-inch-thick pieces (about 1 cup). Transfer the sliced leek to a medium bowl, fill the bowl with cold water, and use your hands to separate the leek pieces and coax out any dirt. Drain through a fine-mesh strainer and repeat this process until there is no dirt left on the leek pieces. Dry the leek pieces well.

3. In a large bowl, combine the bread crumbles, egg, and water. Stir until combined.

4. In a medium skillet over medium heat, warm the vegetable oil until it starts to shimmer. Add the leek and a pinch of salt and pepper and cook, stirring occasionally, until tender, 6 to 8 minutes. Add the garlic and rosemary and cook, stirring constantly, until softened, about 2 minutes. Turn off the heat, stir in the wild rice, and let cool slightly, about 5 minutes.

5. Add the ground turkey to the bowl, then add the mace (if using), 2¾ teaspoons salt, and several large grinds of black pepper. Use your hands to mix until combined. Cover the bowl and refrigerate the filling while you blanch the lettuce leaves and chives.

6. Fill a large, wide skillet with tall sides with water and bring to a boil over medium-high heat. Fill a large bowl with ice water and season the water aggressively with salt (ice bath). Line 2 large plates with paper towels.

7. Once the water reaches a boil, season it aggressively with salt. Working in batches of 2 or 3, add the large romaine leaves to the boiling water. Cook very briefly, until the romaine turns bright green and just wilts, about 2 seconds. Use a slotted spoon to transfer the romaine to the ice bath. Stir several times, until the leaves are no longer hot, then use your hands to gently pick up the leaves and lay them flat on one of the paper towel–lined plates. Repeat with the remaining large romaine leaves, placing a layer of paper towels between each batch of romaine leaves on the first plate.

8. Repeat the process with the romaine strips and stack the strips on the second paper towel–lined plate. Scatter the chives over the boiling water and cook very briefly also, until the chives just wilt, about 2 seconds. Use tongs to transfer the chives to the ice bath (add more ice, if needed), stir several times until they are no longer hot, then transfer to the second paper towel–lined plate, alongside the blanched romaine strips.

9. Preheat the oven to 350°F. Remove the chilled filling from the refrigerator.

10. Lay a large romaine leaf on a cutting board so it is lengthwise in front of you, then add a lettuce strip in the center to fill the gap. Scoop a scant ½ cup of the filling onto the center of the lettuce, then use your hands to press the filling into a 1 by 4-inch log that fits lengthwise on the leaf. Gently pick up the bottom edge of the leaf and tightly fold it over the filling, then fold in the left and right sides of the leaf (similar to wrapping a burrito). Then roll up the leaf until the filling is completely enclosed in the lettuce. If any of the filling leaks out of the lettuce, just patch the gap with an additional lettuce strip. Wrap a chive around the center of the stuffed lettuce leaf and tie a knot to secure the package. (There are several extra chives in case any break during the tying.) Trim the chive knot with kitchen shears if lengthy, then transfer the stuffed lettuce to a 9 by 13-inch baking dish. Repeat to make 11 additional stuffed lettuces, arranging the rolls snugly side by side in the baking dish.

11. Pour the stock over the stuffed lettuces, then dot the tops with the butter. Cover the dish tightly with aluminum foil and bake until the rolls are firm to the touch, about 40 minutes.

12. PREPARE THE GRAVY: In a medium saucepan over medium heat, melt the butter. Add the shallot, season with salt and pepper, and cook, stirring occasionally, until softened, 6 to 8 minutes. Stir in the flour and cook for 3 minutes, stirring constantly. Gradually whisk in 2 cups of the stock and bring to a simmer, 7 to 10 minutes, whisking frequently. Continue to simmer, whisking frequently, until the sauce is thickened to the consistency of gravy and you can no longer taste raw flour, about 10 additional minutes. Whisk in the Worcestershire sauce and season with salt and pepper. (If the gravy is a touch too thick, whisk in a touch of the remaining stock until gravy is your desired consistency.) Pour the gravy into a gravy boat.

13. Transfer the stuffed lettuces to a large serving platter and serve with the gravy on the side.

GREEK-INSPIRED WHOLE LAVRAKI

This impressive dish of a whole branzino adds a stunning touch to a dinner party and satisfies Colin's new liking for fish, post Grecian travels. Purchasing a whole fish is more economical than buying fillets, and the practical Bridgerton cook would have found it ridiculous to spend more for just part of a fish. The fish is stuffed with fresh oregano, along with lemon slices and sliced garlic. It is then drizzled with a vinaigrette made from kalamata olives and cherry tomatoes, and garnished with fresh dill.

Makes 4 servings

6 garlic cloves

8 large sprigs of fresh oregano

12 ounces rainbow cherry tomatoes, halved

½ cup pitted kalamata olives, hand-torn in half

1 small shallot, finely chopped

¼ cup extra-virgin olive oil, plus additional for greasing

2 tablespoons red wine vinegar

¼ teaspoon red pepper flakes

Kosher salt

2 large lavraki (sea bass, also sold as branzino, 1 to 1¼ pounds each), cleaned, scales and fins removed

1 large bunch of fresh dill

1 lemon, sliced into thin half-moons

1. Place a rack on the top shelf of the oven and preheat the oven to 450°F.

2. Finely grate 2 of the garlic cloves and place in a large bowl. Thinly slice the remaining 4 cloves and set aside. Strip the leaves from 2 of the oregano sprigs, coarsely chop them, and add to the bowl with the grated garlic. Add the cherry tomatoes, olives, shallot, 2 tablespoons of the olive oil, the vinegar, red pepper flakes, and a large pinch of salt. Stir to combine.

3. Place a wire rack in a large rimmed baking sheet (sheet pan), then lightly grease the wire rack. Arrange the 2 fish on the rack and make 3 deep, diagonal slashes through the skin on each side of the fish. Rub the inside and outside of the fish with the remaining 2 tablespoons olive oil, then season liberally with salt. Stuff the inside of each fish with some of the garlic slices, the remaining oregano sprigs, the dill (reserve a few fronds for garnish), and the lemon slices.

4. Bake until the fish are browned in spots and just cooked through (flesh should be flaky when turned gently with a fork), about 20 minutes. Taste the marinated tomatoes and olives and season with more salt, if needed. Spoon the marinated tomatoes and olives onto a large serving platter with a slight rim, then place the fish on top. Hand-tear the reserved dill over the top of the fish and serve.

LUSCIOUS LEEKS

———— ⚓ ————

Creamed leeks are a perfect vegetable side dish in a household with children of all ages. While leeks might not be exotic, this simple and flavorful recipe appeals to everyone. During the Middle Ages, it was believed that young girls who slept with a leek under their pillow on Saint David's Day (March 1) would see their future husband in their dreams. A significant side benefit for the husband-hunting ladies of the ton!

Makes 6 to 8 servings

4 extra-large leeks
(about 3½ pounds)

3 tablespoons unsalted butter

Kosher salt and freshly ground
black pepper

⅓ cup vegetable stock

1 dried bay leaf

½ cup heavy cream

⅛ teaspoon mace

½ cup crème fraîche

2 tablespoons coarsely chopped
fresh flat-leaf parsley

1. Trim the roots and tough dark green tops from the leeks, then cut each leek in half lengthwise. Slice each leek half crosswise into ½-inch-thick pieces (about 12 cups). Transfer the sliced leeks to a large bowl, fill the bowl with cold water, and use your hands to separate the leek pieces and coax out any dirt. Drain through a large strainer and repeat this process until there is no dirt left on the leeks. Dry the leeks (a salad spinner works really well), then set aside.

2. In a large Dutch oven or large heavy-bottomed pot set on medium to medium-high heat, melt the butter. Add the leeks, season with salt and pepper, and cook, stirring occasionally, until the leeks are wilted and starting to become tender, about 10 minutes. Add the stock and bay leaf and cook, stirring occasionally, until the stock is reduced by a little more than half, about 5 minutes. Add the cream and mace and cook, stirring occasionally, until the cream is slightly reduced and thickened and the leeks are very tender, about 10 additional minutes. Remove and discard the bay leaf. Remove the pot from the heat and stir in a little more than half of the crème fraîche. (If the sauce is a touch thin, add the remaining crème fraîche, a tablespoon at a time, until it is thick enough to coat the leeks nicely.) Season to taste with additional salt and pepper.

3. Transfer to a large serving bowl, garnish with the chopped parsley, and serve.

The BRIDGERTON FAMILY CHRISTMAS PUDDING

Christmas pudding, or plum pudding, is one of the oldest and most iconic of British recipes. Serving it at dinner parties was a sign of patriotism during the Georgian period, and a family like the Bridgertons would make a point of showing their allegiance to the crown.

The Bridgerton pudding starts on Stir-up Sunday, a few weeks before Christmas. The younger members of the Bridgerton family take turns stirring the pudding mix. They each get to make a wish and add trinkets that bring good luck to whoever finds them in their serving of pudding. Lady Violet loves this tradition and the hustle and bustle it brings to the kitchen, transforming it into the children's domain for that day.

Making the pudding this far in advance allows enough time for its flavor to develop. However, recognizing that many modern cooks may not plan so far ahead, we've devised a recipe that conjures up a perfect pudding in just 24 hours. The suet and alcohol act as a preservative, and the result is a dark and sticky cake with intense flavors of fruit.

Makes 8 to 10 servings

FOR THE PLUM PUDDING

½ cup dried currants

½ cup dried peaches, finely chopped

½ cup raisins, finely chopped

5 large pitted Medjool dates, finely chopped

1 medium navel orange, zested and juiced (about 1 tablespoon zest and ½ cup juice)

½ cup (4 ounces) brandy

¼ cup shredded suet, at room temperature

¼ cup (½ stick) unsalted butter, at room temperature, plus extra for greasing

½ cup (lightly packed) dark brown sugar

½ teaspoon ground cinnamon

¼ teaspoon ground cloves

¼ teaspoon ground ginger

¼ teaspoon ground allspice

¼ teaspoon freshly grated nutmeg

¼ teaspoon mace

Kosher salt

2 large eggs

½ cup all-purpose flour, sifted

½ cup plain dry bread crumbs

¼ cup candied pineapple wedges, finely chopped

¼ cup candied orange peel, finely chopped

½ cup peeled and grated fresh apple, such as Honeycrisp or Fuji

FOR THE BAY LEAF CUSTARD

1 cup heavy cream

½ cup whole milk

2 dried bay leaves

4 large egg yolks

3 tablespoons granulated sugar

SPECIAL EQUIPMENT:
1 (4¼-cup) ceramic pudding basin

recipe continues

COOK'S NOTE: *Suet might seem like a peculiar ingredient to us cooks today, but until baking powder was invented in the mid-nineteenth century, bakers used suet—rendered kidney fat—instead of butter for puddings. When heated, suet created air bubbles in the pudding, giving it a spongy texture rather than being heavy, which is why it is used here. You can ask your butcher for fresh suet and grate it, or you can use shredded suet, a product that is also available. If obtaining suet proves impossible, simply increase the butter by ¼ cup; it will yield a similar result.*

1. MAKE THE PLUM PUDDING: In a medium bowl, combine the currants, peaches, raisins, dates, and orange zest and juice. Pour the brandy over the top, cover the bowl, and let soak overnight at room temperature.

2. In a large bowl, combine the suet, butter, brown sugar, cinnamon, cloves, ginger, allspice, nutmeg, mace, and ¼ teaspoon salt. Use an electric hand mixer on high speed to beat the ingredients until lighter in color and fluffy, about 3 minutes. Beat in the eggs, one at a time, stopping and scraping down the bowl occasionally.

3. Use a rubber spatula to fold the flour into the wet ingredients until just combined and repeat with the bread crumbs. Add the brandy-soaked fruits along with the candied pineapple, orange peel, and grated apple and stir until evenly combined.

4. Grease a 4¼-cup ceramic (or other microwave-safe) pudding basin with a little butter. (Alternatively, use a similar size ceramic bowl that is approximately 6½ inches in diameter and 4 inches tall.) Cut a piece of parchment to line the bottom of the basin. Grease the parchment with more butter.

5. Place a trivet into a large pot with a tight-fitting lid (the pot must be tall enough to fit the pudding basin on top of the trivet and still be covered with the lid).

6. Spoon the pudding into the basin. Cut a round of parchment to fit on top of the batter and butter one side of the parchment. Gently press the parchment buttered side down on top of the pudding. Add another piece of parchment, followed by aluminum foil fitted tightly around the top of the basin. Use kitchen twine to secure the parchment and foil, sealing the pudding.

7. Place the basin on the trivet and add enough water to come halfway up the sides of the basin. Cover the pot and bring the water to a simmer over medium heat (the timing of this will vary depending on the size of your pot). Reduce the heat to low and simmer until the pudding is set, about 6 hours. Maintain the water level in the pot by simmering water in a kettle and refilling as needed. To test for doneness, remove the cover and insert a toothpick or skewer into the center. If it comes out clean, it is done; if not, cover and steam until done.

8. Remove the pudding basin from the simmering water and let cool slightly, enough to handle, 20 to 30 minutes. Remove the top foil and parchment layers. Place a plate on top of the pudding and carefully flip the basin over to release the pudding onto a serving plate. If it sticks, use your fingers to help nudge it out.

9. The pudding is delicious eaten right away, but traditionally it can be made weeks in advance to allow the flavors to mature. To do so, put the pudding back into its basin and close the top tightly with plastic wrap. Store in a cool, dry place for approximately 6 weeks, feeding it with brandy once a week. To do this, remove the plastic wrap, poke a few small holes in the pudding with a skewer and pour 1 to 2 tablespoons of brandy onto the surface. The brandy will penetrate the pudding, adding a little punch. Cover with fresh plastic wrap and repeat each week.

10. To serve the pudding warm, remove the plastic wrap and place it in its basin into the microwave and reheat in 30-second increments. Alternatively, you can rewarm it in the same steamer setup as the pudding was originally cooked in, this time just steaming the pudding until warmed through.

11. Unmold as instructed earlier, flipping the pudding out onto a serving plate.

12. MAKE THE CUSTARD: In a medium saucepan over medium heat, stir together the cream, milk, and bay leaves. Bring the mixture to a simmer, then remove from the heat. Place a fine-mesh strainer over a medium bowl.

13. In another medium bowl, whisk together the egg yolks and sugar until the sugar dissolves and the mixture thickens enough that it falls in ribbon-like ripples back into the bowl, 2 to 3 minutes. Slowly whisk the warm cream mixture into the eggs, whisking constantly, to temper the eggs, then pour the egg-sugar mixture into the saucepan and place over medium-low heat. Cook, stirring constantly, until it thickens into a custard that coats the back of a spoon (approximately 170° to 180°F on an instant-read thermometer), 2 to 5 minutes. Immediately strain the mixture and discard the bay leaves.

14. Serve the plum pudding with the bay leaf custard.

Note: If you are storing the custard, place a piece of plastic wrap directly on the top of the custard and refrigerate for up to 3 days. Reheat by microwaving the custard in 10-second increments, stirring in between, until warmed through.

PLUM PUDDING

In the Regency era, the pudding was wrapped in a cloth and boiled in a large pot of water or even in the washing copper, resulting in a cannonball shape that has become emblematic in British culinary history. When ceramic pudding basins became more common, the pudding was steamed instead. Home cooks can use a traditional pudding basin (a staple in every British home), a sturdy ceramic bowl, or even a decorative cake mold. In the Victorian period, plum puddings molded into shapes like temples and castles were popular, so feel free to unleash your creativity. Slices of leftover pudding were traditionally fried in a pan with plenty of butter, creating an incredibly satisfying dish when paired with a dollop of ice cream. The "plum" in plum pudding refers to raisins, which were known as plums in the Georgian period.

VICTORIA SANDWICH CAKE
for Accomplished Ladies

The Bridgerton family loves their afternoon tea, which is why their side tables are heaped with delicious refreshments for both the family and guests to enjoy. A Victoria sandwich cake can be as simple as a single cake layer with the best jam you have in your cupboard, or it can be enhanced by adding fresh cream and strawberries sandwiched between two layers of cake. Swapping out the jam for lemon curd is equally delicious. Early recipes for this cake were baked in a sheet tray instead of round cake pans, and cut into individual finger-shaped cakes. The cake is an essential component of a traditional British afternoon tea, a habit that, like this cake, became fashionable in the Victorian era.

Makes 8 to 12 servings

1½ cups (3 sticks) unsalted butter, at room temperature, plus additional for greasing

2½ cups self-rising flour

1¾ cups granulated sugar

Kosher salt

6 large eggs, at room temperature

⅓ cup whole milk, at room temperature

⅔ to 1 cup red fruit jam, such as strawberry, raspberry, or red currant

Superfine sugar (also called castor sugar) or confectioners' sugar, for dusting

1. Preheat the oven to 350°F. Grease two 9-inch round cake pans with butter, then line the bottoms with parchment and grease the parchment with more butter.

2. Sift the self-rising flour into a medium bowl.

3. In a large bowl, use an electric hand mixer set on medium-high speed to beat the butter, sugar, and ¼ teaspoon salt until light and fluffy, about 3 minutes. Beat in the eggs, one at a time, stopping and scraping down the bowl occasionally, and adding 1 tablespoon of flour when adding each of the last 2 eggs (this helps the batter to not curdle). Add half the remaining flour and mix on low speed until mostly combined. Drizzle in the milk and add the remaining flour, then mix on low speed until the batter is just combined. It should be smooth but fairly thick.

4. Divide the batter evenly between the 2 cake pans and smooth the tops with a spatula. Bake until the tops are golden brown and a cake tester or toothpick inserted into the center of the cakes comes out clean, about 25 minutes, rotating the cakes

front to back once after 15 minutes. Transfer the cakes to a wire rack to cool briefly, then use a butter knife or small offset spatula to loosen the sides of the cakes from their pans. Cool in the pans for 10 minutes, then carefully remove the cakes, peel off the parchment, and cool completely on the wire rack.

5. Place one of the cakes on a serving plate or cake stand, spread the jam on top (leaving a bit of a border around the edges of the cake), then stack with the second cake (rounded side up). Dust the top of the cake with superfine sugar before slicing into wedges and serving.

PEACH-RHUBARB ADE

———— ♠ ————

The sweet taste of summery peach and the sour hint of rhubarb bring to mind Violet
Bridgerton's childhood birthday parties and the paper crowns her father made for
the occasion. Although Violet prefers the alcohol-free version, the older Bridgerton
boys have been known to add whisky to theirs, to help them graciously navigate all the
matchmaking mamas who pop up in their path.

Makes 6 to 8 servings

3½ cups water, plus additional
if needed

1 pound ripe peaches (about 3),
pitted (reserve the pits) and cut
into roughly 1-inch pieces, plus
additional slices for garnish

8 ounces rhubarb stalks,
trimmed and cut into roughly
½-inch pieces

1¼ cups sugar

½ cup fresh lime juice

Ice cubes, for serving

Lime slices

Mint sprigs, for garnish

COOK'S NOTE: *You can make
the syrup a couple days in advance, so
you need only assemble the drink
before your guests arrive. For a boozy
version, add ½ to 1 cup (4 to
8 ounces) of whisky to the pitcher or
punch bowl of the Peach-Rhubarb
Ade, or add a splash or two to
individual serving cups.*

1. In a medium saucepan over medium heat, stir together 2 cups
of the water, the chopped peaches, peach pits, rhubarb, and sugar,
then bring to a simmer, about 10 minutes. Reduce the heat to low
and continue to simmer, stirring occasionally, until the peaches
and rhubarb are tender, about 10 additional minutes. Remove
from the heat and let cool completely.

2. Remove the pits, then pour the mixture through a fine-mesh
strainer set over a medium bowl, pushing down on the solids
until all the juices have been extracted. (You may have to do this
in batches.) You will be left with about 3½ cups of sweet and
tart, lightly pink peach-rhubarb syrup; you can use the pulp
as a topping for yogurt or to blend into a smoothie or to spread
on toast.

3. In an extra-large pitcher or punch bowl, combine the peach-
rhubarb syrup, the lime juice, and the remaining 1½ cups water.
Taste and adjust with additional water, if needed. Fill the pitcher
with ice cubes, then stir in the peach and lime slices. Pour into
serving glasses or punch glasses and garnish with the mint sprigs,
then serve.

YORKSHIRE-FORCED RHUBARB

The northern region of Yorkshire is
renowned for its stunning, bright pink
rhubarb plants. This sweeter rhubarb
is created through a process known
as forcing, whereby the rhubarb is
grown outdoors for two years,
allowing exposure to frost to fortify
the roots. Then the plants are
carefully dug up and transferred to
dark sheds, where heat is applied,
stimulating rapid growth and
preventing the stalks from turning
sour or bitter. Before they discovered
this way of forcing rhubarb at the end
of the nineteenth century, a lot of
sugar was needed to make the
rhubarb palatable, which meant only
the upper class could afford to spend
the money on sugar for enjoying it.

APPLE *and* THYME TEA PUNCH

—◆—

This thyme-infused apple and English Breakfast tea punch brims with elegance. Often served in a striking glass bowl, the punch is garnished with apples and thyme sprigs and is served at balls and garden parties. Cut-glass punch bowl sets, complete with matching punch glasses and pressed-glass ladles, were a hit during the Regency era and were an essential part of a lady's dowry. The punch bowl sets were passed down through the family, a cherished reminder of many delightful balls.

Makes 6 to 8 servings

3½ cups water

½ cup (packed) light brown sugar

½ teaspoon freshly grated nutmeg, plus additional for garnish

3 large sprigs of fresh thyme, plus smaller sprigs for garnish

4 English Breakfast tea bags (decaf, if preferred)

1 (750ml) bottle sparkling dry or sweet nonalcoholic apple cider

⅓ cup fresh lemon juice

4 to 6 dashes of Angostura bitters

1 small sweet apple, such as Gala, cored and thinly sliced

1 small lemon, cut into thin rounds, for garnish

Ice cubes, for serving

NUTMEG

Ever since the Middle Ages, nutmeg has been a popular spice, and in the Regency era, nutmeg was highly fashionable. The whole nutmeg is the seed of the *Myristica fragrans* tree, which is native to Indonesia. The nutmeg seed is encased in a tasty fruit and seed is itself covered with a rusty orange-red netting that is harvested, dried and ground, then sold as mace. Whole nutmeg seeds are also ground and sold as a spice.

Nutmeg's history as a valuable and expensive spice is intertwined with its scarcity and the competition for control of its trade routes. Because it was scarce, nutmeg became a status symbol in the Regency era. In the eighteenth and nineteenth centuries, it was popular, as a display of one's wealth, for men to carry a fine silver or wooden pocket nutmeg grater and a nutmeg to grate over servings of punch. The men of the ton would have loved to show off their delicate nutmeg graters.

1. In a small saucepan, combine ½ cup of the water, the brown sugar, and ½ teaspoon nutmeg. Working with one large thyme sprig at a time, rub along the stem to strip the leaves with your fingers and let them fall into the water. This will help release some of the plant's essential oils. Heat, stirring frequently, until the sugar is completely dissolved and the mixture is hot and steamy, about 5 minutes. Pour into a small bowl and let cool completely.

2. Meanwhile, in the same saucepan, bring 1½ cups of the water to a boil over medium-high heat, about 3 minutes. Add the tea bags and steep for 5 minutes. Remove and discard the tea bags, then add the remaining 1½ cups water to cool down the tea. Pour the tea into a large punch bowl.

3. Strain and discard the thyme from the syrup and pour it into the cooled tea along with the apple cider, lemon juice, Angostura bitters, apple, lemon, and smaller thyme sprigs. Stir to combine, then fill the punch bowl with ice cubes. Ladle the punch from the top into serving glasses, then garnish with a light grating of nutmeg, and serve.

The FEATHERINGTONS

"You find things to love, my dear."
—LADY FEATHERINGTON

In a feat that would make any mama of the ton proud, Lady Featherington has three happily married daughters, who are now all mothers. Prudence is married to the handsome Harry Dankworth, and Philippa is married to the agreeable Albion Finch. But it is Penelope, the youngest and most overlooked child, who has unexpectedly found true love when she marries her longtime family friend (and crush), Colin Bridgerton. Lady Portia Featherington has newfound respect for her youngest, and the Featheringtons enjoy the merging of their clan with the Bridgertons. This new era of domestic bliss doesn't preclude lavish balls; Prudence and Philippa are as ambitious as ever, wanting to throw the grandest ball that Mayfair has ever seen.

The Featherington dining table is a canvas for Portia's vibrant approach to life. She requires meals with style and verve, instructing her cook to craft colorful dishes that are artfully presented, like the impressive Truly Royal Jelly. In this chapter we also find Salmagundi, which has been the queen of salads for centuries, as well as a festive ham with treacle and roasted figs and a grand and colorful trifle that is no trifling matter. There is, of course, an abundance of cakes and biscuits on the Featherington side table to tempt any esteemed visitors. Portia's commitment is unwavering; she would part with the family's silver candlesticks to ensure her daughters are finely dressed and her tables are perpetually laden with delectable fare.

SALMAGUNDI

———◆———

This cold chicken and anchovy salad is Lady Portia Featherington's pride and joy, and it receives lavish compliments from visitors. Salmagundi is one of the world's oldest named salads, and it serves as the precursor of a beloved contemporary favorite, the Caesar salad. The key to elevating this salad to showstopper status lies in achieving height. Historical recipes suggest placing one or two saucers (which were deeper then) in the middle of a platter and arranging the salad on top and around them. Lady Portia can be heard commanding her cook to make the salad higher, higher than all the salads of London Town! The distinct Portia twist, as one might guess, involves infusing a touch of color by adding bright red beets.

Makes 6 to 8 servings

2 bone-in, skin-on chicken breasts (about 2 pounds total)

Kosher salt and freshly ground black pepper

9 tablespoons red wine vinegar

9 tablespoons extra-virgin olive oil

3 tablespoons water, plus additional if needed

12 ounces red beets, peeled and cut into ½-inch wedges

3 garlic cloves, lightly crushed

3 teaspoons honey, clover or other

½ cup very thinly sliced red onion

1 tablespoon Dijon mustard

4 ounces watercress

4 ounces red butter lettuce

4 hard-boiled large eggs, peeled and quartered lengthwise

1 large ripe but firm Fuyu persimmon (about 8 ounces), peeled and cut into thin wedges

4 radishes, thinly sliced

⅔ cup salted roasted hazelnuts, coarsely chopped

8 to 12 anchovies packed in olive oil, drained and patted dry

COOK'S NOTE: *Owing to the grandeur of this salad, vegetarians can easily omit the meat or fish and even leave out the eggs, should they want to. As the historical recipes also suggest, one can be creative with different types of salad leaves, herbs, and shapes of vegetables, either fresh, cooked, or pickled like capers.*

1. Place the chicken on a small baking sheet and season liberally on all sides with some salt and pepper. Chill, uncovered, in the refrigerator while you roast the beets.

2. Preheat the oven to 375°F.

3. In a 2-quart baking dish, stir together 3 tablespoons of the vinegar, 2 tablespoons of the olive oil, 2 tablespoons of the water, a large pinch of salt, and several grinds of pepper. Add the beets and garlic and gently stir to coat with the liquid. Cover the baking dish with aluminum foil and place in the oven. Roast for 30 minutes, then remove the foil and give the beets a good stir. Continue to roast, uncovered, until the

recipe continues

beets are fork-tender and most of the cooking liquid has been absorbed by the beets, about 30 additional minutes, stirring the beets a couple of times while they cook. Remove the roasted beets from the oven and stir in 1 teaspoon of the honey. Season with more salt and pepper if needed, then set aside to cool completely.

4. Increase the oven temperature to 425°F.

5. Brush the chicken all over with 1 tablespoon of the olive oil and roast until the skin is crisp and golden and an instant-read thermometer inserted into the thickest part of a breast registers 165°F, 30 to 35 minutes, rotating the baking sheet once after 15 minutes. Remove from the oven and let cool slightly.

6. Meanwhile, fill a small bowl with ice water, add the sliced red onion, and soak for 15 minutes.

SALMAGUNDI

The term *salmagundi* is thought to have derived from the sixteenth-century French word *salmigondis*, meaning "a plate of leftover meat" or a "hodgepodge." The recipe first appeared in English in the seventeenth century. Detailed recipes graced cookbooks from the early eighteenth century through the Regency era and up to today, signifying its enduring popularity. Apart from the listed ingredients in this recipe, the salad can be whatever you want it to be, as many of the historical recipes imply. Most use chicken and anchovies, but other recipes include ham, veal, or herring. In many ways, this is also akin to the modern "chopped salad," as a recipe from 1802 instructs to "chop small" all the salad's components.

The first English recipe for this salad in 1707 includes the currently popular barberries for a pop of color and acidity. The recipe gives us instructions on finishing the salad: "Some like it with the Juice of Lemon, and some with Oil and Vinegar beaten up thick together," creating what we know as vinaigrette today.

7. While the onion soaks and the chicken cools, make the dressing. Place 8 of the roasted beet wedges and the roasted garlic in a blender. Use a slotted spoon to scoop the remaining roasted beets into a medium bowl or onto a plate and set aside. Scrape any remaining beet cooking liquid into the blender, then add the mustard, 4 tablespoons of the vinegar, 4 tablespoons of the olive oil, the remaining tablespoon water, and the remaining 2 teaspoons honey. Blend until smooth, then season with salt and pepper. The dressing should be thick but pourable; thin it with a splash of additional water, if needed.

8. Drain the onion, remove any ice cubes, then pat very dry with paper towels. Carefully slice the slightly cooled whole chicken breasts off the bone, then thinly slice both breasts against the grain. In a large bowl, combine the watercress and red butter lettuce. Drizzle with the remaining 2 tablespoons vinegar and 2 tablespoons olive oil, season with salt and pepper, and toss lightly to dress the greens.

9. Transfer the dressed greens to a large serving platter. Working in sections, artfully arrange the chicken slices, roasted beets, and sliced red onion, then the hard-boiled egg quarters, persimmon wedges, sliced radishes, and chopped hazelnuts on top of the dressed greens. Season the eggs with salt and pepper and drape the anchovies over the salad.

10. Present the salmagundi with the beet dressing on the side, then drizzle the salad with the dressing right before serving.

FESTIVE GLAZED HAM

with Treacle and Roasted Figs

———◆———

Ham stands as a classic British celebratory dish, popular at several British holidays and especially at Christmas. With her rapidly multiplying family, Lady Portia Featherington enjoys this tradition when it results in such a splendid dinner table centerpiece that can serve an army. This sweet and sticky ham is served with slow-roasted fruit. In true Regency style, you present the ham elegantly on your best serving platter, surrounded by the fruit. A good hostess shows off the ham to the dinner guests before skillfully carving it, back in the kitchen. And leftovers can be repurposed as delectable sandwiches or transformed into another British classic, ham and fried eggs.

Makes 8 to 10 servings

1 (10- to 12-pound) bone-in ham (not spiral cut and/or seasoned)

1 cup unsweetened pomegranate juice

¼ cup (packed) light brown sugar

¼ cup treacle (see Cook's Note)

2 star anise (optional)

Freshly ground black pepper

3 tablespoons whole-grain mustard

⅓ cup water

2 to 4 tablespoons (1 to 2 ounces) dry white wine

1½ pounds fresh figs, stemmed and halved lengthwise

Pomegranate seeds (arils), for garnish

COOK'S NOTE: *Although not a perfect substitute for black treacle, a blend of equal quantities of blackstrap molasses and honey can be used in its place.*

1. Use a sharp knife to score any fat on the top of the ham in a 1-inch diamond pattern. Let the ham sit at room temperature for 30 minutes.

2. Meanwhile, in a small pot, whisk together the pomegranate juice, brown sugar, treacle, star anise (if using), and several large grinds of black pepper. Bring to a low boil over medium heat, 5 to 8 minutes, whisking occasionally. Lower the heat and simmer, whisking occasionally, until the mixture is reduced by about half, 15 to 20 minutes. Remove from the heat and stir in the mustard.

3. Preheat the oven to 350°F. Place a roasting rack into a large roasting pan and place the ham cut side down on the rack. Pour the water over the ham, cover the roasting pan with aluminum foil, and bake for 1½ hours.

recipe continues

———❀———

THE FEATHERINGTONS

61

4. Remove the foil from the pan (reserve to use later to tent the cooked ham) and brush half the glaze all over the top of the ham. Continue roasting until the ham surface is caramelized and the ham is hot throughout, 1½ to 2 additional hours, basting the ham liberally 4 to 5 additional times with the remaining glaze.

5. Remove the ham from the oven and increase the oven temperature to 375°F. Remove the rack with the ham still on it to a baking sheet or cutting board, and tent with the reserved foil.

6. To the sauce at the bottom of the roasting pan, stir in enough wine to thin it to the consistency of a glossy glaze. Add the figs, stir to combine, then turn so all the figs are cut side up. Place in the oven and roast until the figs are tender and starting to become jammy, about 15 minutes.

7. Slice the rested ham, then transfer the slices to a large platter and arrange the roasted figs around them. Spoon some of the juices from the roasting pan over the slices and garnish with the pomegranate seeds. Serve immediately.

TREACLE

Treacle is an uncrystallized syrup that develops during the sugar-making process. It possesses a thick and dark consistency, coupled with a mildly sweet bitterness, and is commonly recognized as the British equivalent of molasses, albeit with a milder flavor profile. While treacle is frequently used in British baking, it also finds its way into savory dishes. Moreover, treacle takes center stage in a British legend that suggests it isn't derived from sugar factories but, rather, sourced from secret treacle mines.

SOFT-BOILED EGGS
with Anchovy Butter Sippets

———◆———

This delicious and dainty breakfast option is adored by Philippa and Prudence Featherington, who delight in how fancy the eggs are when served. In the grand estates of the ton, boiled eggs arrive at table elegantly carried in beautifully crafted silver egg stands, complete with silver egg cups and matching spoons.

Makes 4 servings

6 tablespoons (¾ stick) unsalted butter, at room temperature

6 anchovies packed in oil, drained and finely minced (about 1 tablespoon)

1 small garlic clove, finely grated

1 tablespoon coarsely chopped fresh flat-leaf parsley

2 teaspoons finely grated lemon zest

1 teaspoon finely chopped fresh tarragon

Pinch of red pepper flakes

Kosher salt

8 large eggs

6 slices white sandwich bread

Flaky sea salt

Freshly ground black pepper

1. Fill a large saucepan two-thirds full with water and bring to a boil.

2. Meanwhile, in a medium bowl, combine the butter, anchovies, garlic, parsley, lemon zest, tarragon, and red pepper flakes. Use a small spatula to stir until smooth. Season to taste with salt, if needed, then cover the bowl and set the anchovy butter aside at room temperature.

3. Once the water is at a boil, use a slotted spoon to gently add the eggs to the boiling water and cook for exactly 6 minutes.

4. While the eggs are cooking, toast the bread slices until lightly browned and very crisp. (The bread should be sturdy so that it will stand up to being dipped into the liquidy egg yolks.) Spread one-sixth of the anchovy butter on one side of each slice. Use a serrated knife to cut away the crust (if desired), then cut each bread slice crosswise into ½-inch-thick strips.

5. Drain and run the eggs under cold running water to stop the cooking process, but only briefly so the eggs remain warm. Dry thoroughly, then place each egg in an egg cup. Divide the eggs evenly among the 4 serving plates (2 eggs each), then arrange the toast sippets alongside the eggs. To eat, the diner gently taps the top of an egg and peels away the top of the shell and sprinkles the egg with some flaky sea salt and black pepper, then dips one of the toast sippets into the yolk.

———✺———

CRAB BISQUE

◆

From the Regency era to the present day, bisque has maintained its status as a luxurious soup, which is why it often appears on Lady Portia's linen-draped table. The traditional French method begins with crafting a *fumet*, or fish stock, which serves as the foundation for the soup. The most important step in creating this soup calls for crushing and frying the shells of crustaceans like lobster, langoustine, shrimp, crayfish, or in this case, crab. Creating such a robust and flavorful concoction from just the shells showcases the true magic of the kitchen.

Makes 4 to 6 servings

3 tablespoons unsalted butter

2 large shallots, finely chopped

2 large celery stalks, trimmed and finely chopped

1 large carrot, peeled and finely chopped

Kosher salt

¼ teaspoon ground white pepper, plus additional to taste

3 garlic cloves, minced

2 tablespoons tomato paste

¾ cup (6 ounces) English dry vermouth or dry white wine

3 tablespoons all-purpose flour

1 quart Crab Stock (recipe follows)

½ cup heavy cream

2 to 2½ cups Dungeness crab meat (from making 1 batch of Crab Stock; see recipe following), picked over for shells and cartilage

Hand-torn fresh chervil or dill, for garnish

COOK'S NOTE: *To save time, you can buy a good-quality seafood stock or make the stock well in advance and freeze it, or, if your household is a small one, you can collect and save the crustacean shells from different meals, adding them to a bag or box you keep in the freezer. When a special occasion arises that calls for bisque, you merely take the shells out of the freezer along with your stock and finish the soup accordingly. Further, for the bisque, you can substitute packaged jumbo lump blue claw or Dungeness crab meat instead of steaming and picking your own crabs.*

1. In a small Dutch oven or heavy-bottomed pot over medium heat, melt the butter. Add the shallots, celery, and carrot, then season with salt and ¼ teaspoon white pepper, and cook, stirring occasionally, until tender, about 15 minutes. Add the garlic and cook, stirring constantly, until softened, about 1 minute more. Add the tomato paste and cook, stirring constantly, for 2 minutes. Add the vermouth and cook, stirring occasionally, until reduced by a little more than half, 6 to 8 minutes. Sprinkle the flour over the vegetables and cook, stirring constantly, for 2 minutes.

2. Stir in the stock and bring to a simmer, 10 to 15 minutes. Continue to cook, stirring occasionally and adjusting the heat as needed to maintain a simmer, until the mixture is thickened and the vegetables are soft enough that you can smash a carrot on the side of the pot, about 25 additional minutes.

recipe continues

3. Transfer the soup to a blender. Depending on the size of your blender, this might have to be done in batches. Remove the cap in the top and place a kitchen towel over the opening (this will allow excess steam to escape during the blending process). Blend the soup until very smooth, then pour it back into the pot. Stir in the cream and taste the bisque for seasoning, adjusting with more salt and white pepper, if needed.

4. Turn the heat to medium and bring the bisque back to a simmer, about 5 minutes, stirring frequently. Gently fold in three-fourths of the crab meat and cook until the crab is just warmed through, 2 to 3 minutes.

5. Ladle the hot bisque into serving bowls and top with the remaining crab meat. Garnish with the chervil and serve immediately.

CRAB STOCK
Makes about 2 quarts stock (and 1 1/2 pounds crab meat)

3 large live Dungeness crabs
(about 2 pounds each)

1 tablespoon vegetable oil

1 large yellow onion, coarsely
chopped

2 large celery stalks, trimmed and
coarsely chopped

1 fennel bulb, trimmed and
coarsely chopped

1 tablespoon tomato paste

3 quarts water

2 dried bay leaves

2 tablespoons black peppercorns

1. Fit a steamer insert into a large stockpot and fill the pot with 2 inches of water, then bring to a boil over medium-high heat. Add the crabs, laying them in the steamer insert (depending on the size of your steamer, you might need to cook the crabs in batches), and cook until the shells are bright red, about 20 minutes. Remove the crabs from the steamer and allow to cool just enough so that they can be handled.

2. Clean the stockpot. Fill a large bowl halfway with ice, then set a medium bowl on top of the ice cubes.

3. Crack the shells and carefully remove the meat from the crab legs, claws, and bodies, leaving the meat in as large lumps as possible; you should have 1¼ to 1½ pounds of crab meat. As you remove the meat, place it in the bowl set over ice to keep it cold. Reserve the shells in another bowl. Transfer the crab meat to an airtight container and refrigerate; use within 3 days.

4. Remove the spongy gills and guts from the crab bodies, then rinse under cold water until clean. Use your hands to crack the bodies into several pieces (or use a sharp knife) and place in the bowl with the rest of the shells; you should have about 2 pounds of shells. Chill the shells in the refrigerator while you get started on the stock.

5. Place the stockpot on medium heat and add the oil. When oil is shimmering, add the onion, celery, and fennel, and cook, stirring frequently, until crisp-tender, 6 to 8 minutes. Add the tomato paste and cook, stirring constantly, for 1 minute more. Then add the crab shells and use a potato masher to smash them into smaller pieces. Stir the shells so they are mixed with the vegetables and tomato paste and cook, stirring constantly, until the shells are lightly toasted, 3 to 5 minutes.

6. Pour in the water, add the bay leaves and black peppercorns, stir to combine, and bring to a simmer, about 15 minutes. Continue to cook for an additional 30 minutes, then remove from the heat.

7. Place a large fine-mesh strainer over a large bowl or another large pot. Wet a couple layers of cheesecloth and drape them over the strainer. Ladle the hot stock into the strainer, then discard the solids. The stock can be used immediately or cooled completely and transferred to storage containers to be refrigerated for up to 5 days or frozen for up to 6 months.

COUSIN JACK'S ROASTED CORNISH GAME HENS

◆

After the untimely death of Lord Archibald Featherington, the Featherington women find themselves without a lord and without a penny. Enter the new Lord Featherington, the handsome cousin Jack, who moves into Portia's quarters and installs an endless collection of hunting rifles and trophies. One can only hope he is capable of bagging enough game birds for a delicious dinner of roasted Cornish game hens.

Makes 4 servings

1 tablespoon dry mustard

1 tablespoon smoked paprika

1 tablespoon granulated garlic

1 tablespoon light brown sugar

2 teaspoons ground coriander

2 teaspoons coarsely ground pink peppercorns

2 teaspoons coarsely ground fennel seeds

1 teaspoon onion powder

4 Cornish hens (about 1½ pounds each), any livers and gizzards removed

Kosher salt

1½ tablespoons vegetable oil

Fresh hardy herbs, such as thyme, rosemary, and/or sage, for garnish

COOK'S NOTE: *If you cannot acquire game birds, a small chicken can be used instead. The success of this dish depends on the spice rub, which transforms the plainest of meats into something truly flavorful.*

1. In a small bowl, stir together the mustard, paprika, granulated garlic, brown sugar, coriander, pink peppercorns, fennel seeds, and onion powder.

2. Line a large rimmed baking sheet (sheet pan) with foil, then top with a wire rack. Use paper towels to pat the Cornish game hens dry inside and out, then arrange them on the rack. Season the hens inside and out liberally with salt, then sprinkle evenly with the spice rub. Use kitchen twine to tie the legs of each hen together and tuck the wings underneath. Chill, uncovered, in the refrigerator for at least 12 hours and up to 48 hours. The longer you dry-brine the birds, the more flavorful they will be and the skin will crisp up better.

3. Preheat the oven to 425°F.

4. Brush the outsides of the hens lightly with the vegetable oil, smoothing down the spice rub with the pastry brush. Roast the hens until the skin is deeply browned and an instant-read thermometer inserted into the thigh registers 170°F, about 40 minutes, rotating the baking sheet once after 20 minutes.

5. Let the hens rest for 10 minutes, then transfer to a platter. Scatter the herbs about the hens and serve.

TRUE LOVE BISCUITS

———◆———

Although they have existed with the iconic brand name Jammie Dodgers for sixty years, these cookies can be spotted in the world of Bridgerton. These biscuits consist of two pieces of espresso-flavored shortbread sandwiching a layer of red currant jelly. The jelly can be seen through a heart-shaped window in the top biscuit. Feel free to experiment with jellies of different colors—be creative. These picturesque and romantic biscuits are a favorite of Colin and Penelope, when they have an intimate tea for two.

Makes 12 biscuits

1⅓ cups all-purpose flour, plus additional for dusting

¼ cup cornstarch

½ cup granulated sugar

1 tablespoon instant espresso powder

Kosher salt

½ cup (1 stick) unsalted butter, at room temperature

1 large egg

⅓ cup red currant jelly

¼ cup confectioners' sugar

SPECIAL EQUIPMENT:
1 (2½-inch) round or fluted cookie cutter and 1 (1- to 1¼-inch) heart-shaped cookie cutter

COOK'S NOTE: *For a sweet twist on these True Love Biscuits, dust the tops with a couple tablespoons of confectioners' sugar before you press them into the jelly.*

1. In a small bowl, whisk together the flour and cornstarch.

2. In a large bowl, combine the granulated sugar, espresso powder, ¼ teaspoon salt, and the butter. Use an electric hand mixer on medium-high speed to blend the mixture until smooth and lightly fluffy, about 3 minutes. Add the egg and blend again until smooth. Then add the flour and cornstarch mixture and blend on low speed until just combined and a soft, smooth dough forms.

3. Turn out the dough onto a large sheet of parchment and press into a small rectangle about ½ inch thick. Top with a second sheet of parchment and roll out the dough until it is about ⅛ inch thick. Stack 2 baking sheets on top of each other, then slide the parchment layers, with the dough between them, onto the top baking sheet. Chill the dough in the refrigerator until firm, about 30 minutes. By chilling both baking sheets now, you will have 2 equally chilled sheets ready for baking the biscuits.

4. Slide the dough "package" off the baking sheet and onto a work surface. Have a plate nearby with some flour in it. Remove the top sheet of parchment and use it to line the top baking sheet (if any cookie dough is stuck onto it, use a small offset spatula to

recipe continues

scrape it off). Dip a 2½-inch round or fluted cookie cutter into the flour, then use it to cut out rounds from the dough, re-rolling the trimmings as necessary to get 24 biscuits. If the dough starts to become too soft at any point, chill it briefly in the refrigerator until firm enough to again cut out and re-roll. Lay the biscuits in a single layer on the parchment-lined baking sheet; they can be close together because you will be dividing the dough between the 2 baking sheets later. Again, place the stacked baking sheets in the refrigerator and chill until the dough is firm again, about 30 minutes.

5. After 15 minutes, preheat the oven to 350°F.

6. Remove the 2 baking sheets from the refrigerator. Use the top parchment sheet to line the second baking sheet. Then transfer half the biscuits (12) onto that second baking sheet, spacing the biscuits evenly apart. Place one baking sheet of biscuits back in the refrigerator; these are the bottom biscuits. Use the 1- to 1¼-inch heart-shaped cookie cutter to cut out a heart from the center of the remaining 12 biscuits; these are the top biscuits.

7. Bake the sheet of top biscuits until firm and the tops and edges go from shiny to matte, 12 to 14 minutes, rotating the baking sheet once after 6 minutes. Let the biscuits cool completely on the baking sheet. Repeat, baking the bottom biscuits the same way, and let cool on the baking sheet.

8. Turn the 12 bottom biscuits so the flat bottoms are facing up. In a small bowl, whisk the jelly until it is smooth, then spread a heaping teaspoon on each bottom biscuit, leaving a ¼-inch border around the edge. Sift confectioners' sugar to coat the tops of the top biscuits. Lay the top biscuits on the jelly and gently press down to sandwich them together.

ROSE BISCUITS

———◆———

Rose Biscuits resemble the Italian savoiardi biscuits, now more commonly referred to as ladyfingers. They are frequently observed in the Featherington drawing room, where Philippa and Prudence Featherington engage in almost-always ladylike gossip over a plate of these pretty pink treats. Fragile in nature and flavored with a hint of rosewater, these biscuits are visually striking with their pink hue and white sugar-coated tops. While perfect served alongside a cup of tea and accompanying gossip, these fragrant biscuits can also be festively paired with a glass of Champagne at a party.

Makes about 20 biscuits

½ cup cornstarch

½ teaspoon baking powder

½ teaspoon baking soda

¾ cup all-purpose flour, sifted

2 large eggs, whites and yolks separated

½ cup granulated sugar

2 drops pink gel food coloring, plus additional as needed

2 teaspoons rosewater

Kosher salt

¼ cup confectioners' sugar

SPECIAL EQUIPMENT:
1 piping bag fitted with a ½-inch straight piping tip

1. Place a rack on the upper third and another on the lower third of the oven and preheat the oven to 350°F. Line 2 baking sheets with parchment.

2. Sift the cornstarch, baking powder, and baking soda into a large bowl. Add the flour, then whisk to combine.

3. In the bowl of a stand mixer fitted with the whisk attachment, whip the egg whites on medium-high speed until frothy, about 1 minute. Add half the granulated sugar and continue to whip until stiff peaks form, 5 to 7 minutes. Transfer the whites to a medium bowl.

4. To the mixer bowl (no need to clean it out) add the egg yolks, the remaining granulated sugar, the pink food coloring, rosewater, and a pinch of salt. Whip on medium-high speed until smooth and creamy, 2 to 3 minutes.

5. Use a rubber spatula to fold half the whites into the egg yolk mixture. Add the remaining whites and fold until just combined. Repeat this with the flour mixture, adding it in 2 parts and folding it into the batter until just combined, with no white

recipe continues

———✿———

streaks. The batter will have a blush pink tone and a sticky texture. If you want a more vibrant shade of pink, fold in another drop or two of food coloring. Transfer the batter to a piping bag fitted with a ½-inch straight piping tip.

6. Pipe 3½-inch long strips of the batter onto the baking sheets, leaving 2 inches space around each biscuit to allow for spreading; you should have about 10 strips per baking sheet. Bake until the biscuits are just set and dry, 15 to 18 minutes; be careful to not overbake or the biscuits will start to brown. Remove the baking sheets from the oven and turn the oven off.

7. Immediately dust the tops of the biscuits with the confectioners' sugar, then place the baking sheets back in the oven, leaving the door slightly ajar. Let the cookies sit in the cooling oven until completely cooled, 30 minutes to 1 hour. Serve immediately or store in an airtight container at room temperature for up to 3 days.

A TRULY ROYAL JELLY

—◆—

"Let us plan the greatest wedding Mayfair has ever seen."
—PENELOPE FEATHERINGTON

The culinary trends of the Regency era favored recipes that made an impression and added a touch of drama. Lady Featherington, well acquainted with the art of theatrics, is renowned for presenting jellies that could rival those crafted by the esteemed royal chef. This fruit-filled jelly serves as a stunning addition to any party table, especially when illuminated by the light coming in a side window.

Makes 8 to 10 servings

Vegetable oil, for greasing

⅔ cup (about 5 ounces) Pimm's No. 1 Cup liqueur

1 cup sugar

4 (¼-ounce) envelopes unflavored powdered gelatin

1 (750ml) bottle brut rosé Champagne, chilled

Red food coloring (optional)

12 ounces small strawberries (about 24), hulled and halved, plus additional hulled whole berries for garnish

8 ounces small red Champagne grapes, stemmed and halved (about 1¾ cups), plus additional grapes with stems for garnish

2 cups sliced ripe stone fruits, such as mango, apricots, or nectarines, plus additional for garnish

SPECIAL EQUIPMENT:
1 (10-cup) jelly mold or Bundt pan

COOK'S NOTE: *You can use a jelly mold, a Bundt pan, or even a castle-shaped tin if you happen to have one. Alternatively, a large bowl with the 10-cup capacity will suffice. If you are unable to purchase Pimm's No. 1 Cup liqueur, you can substitute an equal mix of good-quality gin, red vermouth, and clear Curaçao or Cointreau.*

1. Lightly dip a folded paper towel into the vegetable oil and wipe a 10-cup jelly mold or Bundt pan with the oil, making sure to get into the crevices or corners if your mold or pan has an intricate design.

2. In a medium saucepan, combine the Pimm's and ⅓ cup of the sugar. Whisk until the sugar is dissolved. Sprinkle the gelatin over the mixture and let it sit until the gelatin is softened, 2 to 3 minutes. Add the remaining ⅔ cup sugar and warm over low heat, whisking occasionally, until the gelatin and sugar are dissolved, 5 to 7 minutes.

3. Pour the gelatin mixture into a large bowl and whisk several times to cool the mixture slightly. Whisk in the Champagne; the mixture should become a light shade of pink, depending on the color of wine used. (If you would prefer a deeper shade of pink, stir in several drops of red food coloring.) Refrigerate, stirring every 10 minutes,

recipe continues

until the gelatin begins to thicken but is still somewhat liquidy, with some small gelled bits, 30 to 50 minutes. The timing of this will vary greatly depending on the temperature of your refrigerator. Foam may appear at the top of the gelatin and that is okay, but if it starts to become opaque and clumpy, use a spoon to skim the clumps so it does not make the gelatin cloudy.

4. To the thickened the gelatin, add the halved strawberries, the grapes, and stone fruit of choice, gently folding in with a rubber spatula. Spoon the semi-firm gelatin and fruit into the mold and give it several stirs to ensure the fruit is well distributed. Flatten the top to make sure all the fruit is submerged in the gelatin. Chill, uncovered, in the refrigerator until firmly set, at least 6 hours and up to overnight.

5. To remove the jelly from the mold, use wet fingers to loosen the sides of the mold and then carefully invert the mold onto a large serving platter, letting the jelly relax gently onto the surface. This step can take some time, but if the jelly does not come out after 5 minutes of trying, fill a wide pot or bowl (anything wider than the mold) with warm water. Dip the mold in the warm water for 5 seconds, then lift out and dry the outside. Quickly and carefully invert the mold, lowering the jelly onto the serving platter. You may have to repeat the dipping a couple of times, until the jelly edges release from the mold. Garnish the jelly with more slices of fresh fruit, then slice and serve.

JELLY MOLDS

During the Georgian period, it was fashionable to create jellies in dramatically shaped molds to encase fruits and vegetables. Special copper molds were crafted, each one more detailed and costly than the last. The Featherington family's cook from that era would have spent hours boiling down and clarifying her homemade jelly.

BATTENBERG CAKE

◆

With its pink and yellow squares and its marzipan jacket, this colorful cake radiates Featherington flair. Indeed, it is the perfect dish to fuel an all-afternoon Penelope and Eloise tête-à-tête. Cakes of this kind can have as many as twenty-five squares, but the four squares in this cake are delightful and easily managed.

Makes 8 servings

¾ cup unsalted butter, at room temperature, plus extra for greasing

1 cup granulated sugar

1 teaspoon vanilla extract

3 large eggs

Yellow gel food coloring, as needed

Pink gel food coloring, as needed

1¼ cups all-purpose flour, sifted

½ cup superfine almond flour

1½ teaspoons baking powder

1 cup apricot preserves

1 (1-pound) block white marzipan

Confectioners' sugar, for dusting

Sugar pearls (optional)

COOK'S NOTE: *If you can find only natural-color marzipan, you can add a few drops of white gel food coloring and knead the marzipan until the dye is evenly incorporated. Add more white dye as needed until you get the right color. Use food-safe gloves to avoid dyeing your hands during this process.*

1. Preheat the oven to 350°F. Grease the bottom and sides of an 8-inch square baking dish with butter. Line the bottom of the pan with parchment.

2. Tear a 12-inch square of heavy-duty aluminum foil. Make a 1½-inch fold along one end of the foil. Continue to fold the foil over itself until you have a 12 by 1½-inch strip of foil. Place the foil strip on a flat surface and use your hands to flatten and smooth it out. Grease the foil on both sides with butter.

3. Place the foil strip upright on its edge and running down the center of the baking dish to create 2 equal sections of the baking pan. Fold the excess foil at the bottom edge to the left and bend the excess at the top edge to the right, so the folded edges are pressed against the opposite sides of the pan. This will keep the 2 batters separate when baking.

4. In a large bowl, combine the butter and granulated sugar. Use an electric hand mixer on medium-high speed to beat the butter and sugar until lighter in color and fluffy, 3 to 4 minutes. Add the vanilla and beat in the eggs, one at a time, stopping and scraping down the bowl after each addition.

recipe continues

5. Divide the batter equally between 2 medium bowls. In one of the bowls, use the hand mixer on medium speed to blend in the yellow food coloring until the batter turns a bright golden hue (2 to 4 drops, depending on the brand). Clean the beaters, then blend the pink food coloring into the other bowl until it turns a vibrant pink (2 to 4 drops, depending on the brand).

6. In a large bowl, whisk together the all-purpose flour, almond flour, and baking powder, breaking up any clumps in the almond flour. Divide the flour mixture evenly between the 2 bowls of batter. Use a different rubber spatula for each bowl to fold the flour into the batter, forming 2 thick batters. Pour the yellow batter into half of the baking pan, spreading it from edge to edge and smoothing the top, then repeat with the pink batter.

7. Bake until the cakes puff and a toothpick inserted into the center of each cake comes out clean, about 40 minutes, rotating the baking dish once after 20 minutes. Let the cakes cool for 10 minutes, then carefully remove the foil divider, and invert the cakes onto a clean work surface. Remove the parchment from the bottoms and place the cakes on a wire rack to cool completely, about 1 hour.

8. Place one of the cakes on a cutting board. Use a serrated knife to trim the domed top and the rounded sides, so that you are left with an 8 by 3-inch cake with straight sides. Repeat with the other piece of cake. Then cut each cake in half lengthwise to make 2 strips that are 8 by 1½ inches, 4 pieces total.

9. Gently heat the apricot preserves in a small saucepan or in the microwave until slightly warmed and with a loosened consistency. Press the preserves through a mesh strainer to remove any lumps. Keep the preserves warm, as this will make it easier to brush onto the cake.

10. The Battenberg cake is assembled by stacking the strips of cake in a way that will show a checkered pattern. The warmed preserves hold the layers together. Start by brushing the inside edge of one strip of yellow and one strip of pink cake with a layer of the preserves. Gently press the 2 strips together. You now have a cake layer measuring 8 by 3 inches. Brush the top of the cake layer with more preserves, and then repeat this process with the remaining 2 strips, reversing the colors of cake and placing the second layer on top of the first layer. Now you have a 2-layer cake measuring 8 by 3 inches.

11. Next, the cake is covered with a thin layer of marzipan that wraps around the cake but leaves the sides exposed. Measure the width of the top of the cake and measure the height of the assembled cake, then double both those amounts and add those measurements together—for example, 3 + 3 (top and bottom widths) + 1½ + 1½ (height of sides) = 9. Your total could be slightly different depending on how much you trimmed your cake. Next, measure the length of your cake; it should be close to the previously trimmed 8 inches. Again, this could be slightly different depending on how much you trimmed the cake.

12. The marzipan is then rolled out and cut to fit your measurements. For example, suppose your cake dimensions are 9 by 8 inches. Dust a clean work surface with confectioners' sugar and roll the marzipan into a ⅛-inch-thick piece that is slightly larger than your dimensions. Use a ruler and paring knife to cut the marzipan to exactly fit the 9 by 8-inch measurements for your cake, being sure to cut the marzipan so it has straight edges.

13. To finish assembling the cake, brush the top of the cake with the preserves. Carefully pick the cake up and flip it over, placing the preserve-coated side down, in the center of the marzipan. The short sides of the cake will line up exactly with the 8-inch edge of marzipan. Brush the 9-inch lengths of the cake and the top with the remaining preserves (there is no need to brush the two shorter sides, as they will not be covered with marzipan). Working with one edge at a time, lift the marzipan and press it up the sides of the cake and then fold it over the top. Repeat this on the other side. The marzipan should cover the cake, with the edges meeting at the top center, without any overlap. (If you do have some excess, use kitchen shears to trim it.) If needed, trim any excess marzipan off the shorter sides as well. The cake should be exposed on both shorter sides, with the marzipan just reaching the edges. Flip the cake back over so the seam side is now down. Use a plastic scraper or fondant tool to gently smooth the marzipan on the top and along the sides of the cake.

14. Transfer the cake to a serving platter. To decorate, use the edge of a ruler or a bamboo skewer to gently score a series of diamond patterns into the top of the marzipan. Place the sugar pearls (if using) where the diamonds intersect. Slice and serve.

15. Any leftover cake can be covered with plastic wrap and held in the refrigerator for up to 3 days.

A GRAND TRIFLE

———◆———

Trifle is another quintessential British classic that gained popularity during the Regency era owing to its impressive presentation, which guarantees it will truly stand out on a crowded table. While the earliest trifles were simple, they began to take on grander forms with more and more layers. Indeed, when it comes to trifle, the principle of "more is more" prevails. The beauty of this recipe is that any seasonal fruit can be used, making it a versatile dish that can be enjoyed by the Featherington sisters all year round.

Makes 10 to 12 servings

FOR THE PAVLOVAS

2 large egg whites, at room temperature

¼ teaspoon cream of tartar

½ cup superfine sugar

½ teaspoon fresh lemon juice

2 teaspoons cornstarch

FOR THE VANILLA PASTRY CREAM

3 cups whole milk

1 tablespoon vanilla extract

6 large egg yolks

⅔ cup granulated sugar

¼ cup cornstarch

Kosher salt

3 tablespoons unsalted butter, cut into cubes

FOR THE RASPBERRY WHIPPED CREAM

2 cups heavy cream

2 tablespoons confectioners' sugar, sifted

¾ cup freeze-dried raspberries, ground or crushed into a fine powder

FOR ASSEMBLY

1 cup peach or apricot preserves

12 slices Charlotte Royale cake (page 222)

¾ cup toasted sliced almonds, plus additional for garnish

¼ cup (2 ounces) dry Champagne or sparkling white wine

12 Rose Biscuits (page 77)

1 cup fresh raspberries, plus additional for garnish

1 cup fresh blueberries, plus additional for garnish

Fresh basil or mint leaves, for sprinkling

SPECIAL EQUIPMENT:
1 (4-quart) trifle dish; 1 piping bag fitted with a ½-inch star tip

COOK'S NOTE: *The trifle can be made up to 4 hours in advance and kept loosely covered in the refrigerator. Do not add the basil or mint until right before serving. Although this recipe shows you how to build a truly show-stopping trifle, do not feel you have to make everything from scratch. You can substitute your favorite store-bought cake, ladyfingers, and meringues in place of the Charlotte Royale cake, Rose Biscuits, and pavlovas. Vanilla pudding (or powdered custard) and whipped cream can also be substituted for the homemade versions featured here.*

recipe continues

1. MAKE THE PAVLOVAS: Place a rack in the upper third and a rack in the lower third of the oven and preheat the oven to 325°F. Line 2 baking sheets with parchment.

2. In the bowl of a stand mixer fitted with the whisk attachment, whip the egg whites on medium-high speed until frothy, about 1 minute. Add the cream of tartar and continue to mix until soft peaks form, about 2 minutes. With the mixer still running at medium-high speed, slowly add the superfine sugar, 1 tablespoon at a time, until it is incorporated and stiff peaks form, 6 to 7 minutes. Turn the mixer off, add the lemon juice, and sift in the cornstarch. Whip again on medium-high speed for 30 seconds to quickly and evenly distribute the lemon juice and cornstarch.

3. Transfer the meringue to a large piping bag fitted with a ½-inch star tip. Pipe 1 circle, 4 inches in diameter, on one of the baking sheets. Pipe the outer circle first, then continue making circles, piping toward the center to form a mound that looks similar to the top of a cupcake. Repeat this process to make 3 additional 4-inch pavlovas, leaving 1 inch of space between each one. Pipe 4 additional pavlovas on the second baking sheet in the same manner. If desired, make a small depression in the tops of the pavlovas, or leave them as is. (Alternatively, for a more rustic look, spoon eight 4-inch mounds of meringue on the baking sheets. Use the back of a spoon to make a large depression at the top of each mound.) Fresh berries can be added to these depressions later, as you are putting together the finished trifle.

4. Place the baking sheets in the oven and immediately reduce the oven heat to 225°F. Bake until the pavlovas are set and dry to the touch, about 1 hour 30 minutes. Turn the oven off and leave the pavlovas in the oven to cool completely, 1 to 2 hours.

5. MAKE THE PASTRY CREAM: In a large saucepan on medium to medium-high heat, combine the milk and vanilla and bring to a simmer, stirring frequently to prevent the milk from scorching, about 5 minutes. Turn off the heat and cover with a lid to keep warm. Place a fine-mesh strainer over a medium bowl and fill a large bowl halfway with ice cubes and cold water (an ice bath).

6. In the bowl of a stand mixer fitted with a whisk attachment, combine the egg yolks, granulated sugar, cornstarch, and ¼ teaspoon salt and whip on high speed until it doubles in size and becomes pale yellow in color, about 2 minutes.

7. With the mixer on low speed, gradually add the warm vanilla milk to the egg yolk mixture. Do not rush this process or you will scramble the eggs. When all the milk has been added, pour the mixture back into the saucepan and cook over medium-low heat, gently whisking constantly, until the mixture thickens to the consistency of pudding and you just begin to see bubbles reach the surface, about 3 minutes. Turn the heat off and stir in the butter, 2 to 3 pieces at a time, until the pastry cream is smooth and glossy. Strain through the fine-mesh strainer to remove any lumps, then place the bowl of pastry cream into the ice bath and stir until the cream is completely cooled. If not using right away, cover with plastic wrap directly on the surface of the pastry cream and refrigerate for up to 3 days.

8. MAKE THE WHIPPED CREAM: In the bowl of a stand mixer fitted with the whisk attachment, combine the cream and confectioners' sugar. Whip on high speed until soft peaks form, 2 to 3 minutes. Remove the whisk attachment and use a rubber spatula to gently fold in the freeze-dried raspberries. Cover with plastic wrap and refrigerate until ready to use; it will keep nicely for up to 2 hours, but any longer and the cream might begin to weep.

9. ASSEMBLE THE TRIFLE AND SERVE: Spread the preserves in the bottom of a 4-quart trifle dish. Arrange 7 or 8 of the cake slices vertically on top of the preserves so that the cake slices stand up (swirled side facing out) and they line the entire edge of the trifle dish. Lay the remaining slices horizontally in the center of the dish on top of the preserves.

10. Dollop the pastry cream over the top of the cake slices and use a rubber spatula to spread it in an even layer; it is okay if some of the pastry cream drips down into the cake layer. Sprinkle the toasted almonds evenly over the top of the pastry cream.

11. Brush the Champagne onto the rose biscuits, then arrange most of the biscuits evenly on top of the almonds. Set any extra biscuits on their side along the outer edge of the dish so that the tops face out.

12. Dollop the raspberry whipped cream over the biscuits and use a rubber spatula to spread it into an even layer. Sprinkle the fresh raspberries and blueberries evenly over the whipped cream. Stack the mini pavlovas on top of the whipped cream and berries. Garnish the top of the trifle with additional fresh berries and toasted almonds. Sprinkle with the basil or mint leaves and serve immediately.

TRIFLE

Though the first trifle recipe appeared in the sixteenth century, trifle has evolved into a multilayered delight, including a jelly layer suggested by cookbook author Hannah Glasse in 1760. She refers to it as a "grand trifle," and her creation has served as an inspiration for trifle variations for years. Although a trifle is often likened to an Italian tiramisu today, it's worth noting that the trifle was the precursor of the tiramisu, the latter which emerged only in the 1960s.

A DISCREET PUNCH

———◆———

While punch traditionally dilutes strong liquors, it also doesn't need to be overly alcoholic. This red wine and currant punch incorporates only a modest amount of brandy and wine. The resulting fragrant beverage with notes of honey, sugar, cinnamon, cloves, and orange is perfect for Philippa and Prudence Featherington, who can otherwise get particularly voluable after over-imbibing at a ball.

Makes 6 to 8 servings

½ cup water

¼ cup honey

¼ cup sugar

4 cinnamon sticks

12 whole cloves

⅔ cup (about 5 ounces) brandy

2 (750ml) bottles full-bodied dry red wine, such as Cabernet Sauvignon

1½ cups black currant juice

1 cup fresh tangerine juice

2 small tangerines or mandarins

6 ounces fresh red currants

Ice cubes, for serving

COOK'S NOTE: *If fresh red currants are out of season or prove hard to find, you can substitute another small red berry, such as raspberries, for garnish.*

1. In a small saucepan set over medium heat, stir together the water, honey, sugar, cinnamon sticks, and cloves and bring to a simmer, stirring occasionally, about 5 minutes. Remove from the heat and let cool completely at room temperature. Once cooled, stir in the brandy, then strain through a fine-mesh strainer into a large punch bowl (discard the spices). Add the wine, currant juice, and tangerine juice and stir to combine. Cover the bowl with plastic wrap and chill in the refrigerator for at least 2 hours and up to 5 days.

2. When ready to serve, slice the tangerines or mandarins crosswise into thin rounds and separate the currants into small clusters. Fill the bowl of punch with ice cubes, then stir in the tangerine slices and red currants. Ladle the punch into glasses and serve.

PUNCH

Like many aspects of history, the origins of punch are shrouded in obscurity, surrounded by a multitude of theories. A prevailing notion is that the term *punch* originates from the Hindi word for "five," alluding to the five essential ingredients in a traditional punch: alcohol, water, sour, sugar, and spice. However, punch often includes more or fewer elements. Another theory suggests that the word derives from *puncheon*, the term for a small 50-liter barrel. What remains certain is that starting from the 1660s, punch became the favored beverage among English aristocrats and served as a lucrative avenue for London's coffeehouses to generate income, as they weren't subjected to taxes on punch sales.

MADAME DELACROIX'S MELON
Draped in French Ham

◆

"I happen to believe a lady's business is her own."
—MADAME DELACROIX

Madame Delacroix runs her own modiste business, while also relishing the pleasures
of nightlife with her friends and potential suitors. As a woman working for herself,
she leads a busy life that affords little time for cooking. Lacking a cook of her own,
perhaps she enjoys simple but elegant fare, like this melon draped with ham (much
like the exquisite fabrics she uses to drape the ton). During the Regency era, melons
cultivated in English greenhouses were considered status symbols, so this recipe
would be a sweet indulgence for a successful woman.

Makes 6 to 8 servings

½ small ripe cantaloupe
(about 2 pounds)

½ small ripe honeydew melon
(about 2 pounds)

1 tablespoon raspberry or
Champagne vinegar

1 tablespoon honey

Kosher salt and freshly ground
black pepper

16 to 20 thin slices Jambon
de Bayonne or prosciutto
(6 to 8 ounces)

Micro radish greens,
for garnish

COOK'S NOTE: *Clever presentation can transform a simple recipe into a beautiful and elegant dish for
any dinner party. The combination of the sweetest melon and the most luxurious ham you can afford makes this
dish truly shine. Incorporating small extras, such as delicate microgreen leaves and colorful raspberry vinegar,
enhances the visual appeal. To elevate this simple dish to a Bridgerton level, choose your most exquisite-looking
plate or use a cake stand for serving.*

1. Place a fine-mesh strainer over a medium bowl, then scoop the seeds from the
melons (along with all the juices) into the strainer. Use the back of a spoon or rubber
spatula to press down on the seeds to extract as much additional juice as possible.
Discard the seeds and set the melon juice aside. Peel the melon halves, cut each into
8 to 10 wedges (about ¾ inch thick), and transfer to a large baking dish.

2. To the melon juice, add the vinegar, honey, a pinch of salt, and several large grinds
of black pepper. Whisk to combine, then drizzle over the melon wedges. Gently turn to
coat, then chill in the refrigerator for 1 hour, turning the melons once after 30 minutes.

3. Drape a slice of ham around each wedge of juicy melon, arrange on a large serving
platter, and garnish with the radish greens.

❈

Lady
DANBURY

*"I have loved. I have lost. I have
earned the right to do whatever I
please, whenever I please, and
however I please to do it."*
—LADY DANBURY

Lady Danbury's life experience has
given her wisdom and a permanent
place in the ton. Her position is hard
won, and the mature Lady Danbury
does not compromise on happiness;
she is a woman who knows what she
wants and does what she wants. But
underneath her formidable exterior,
she is a generous, intelligent friend and
a canny, loving sponsor to the Duke of
Hastings.

When the hustle and bustle of
the ton have left her grand home,
Lady Danbury prefers the intimacy of
small bites, like Devils on Horseback
or English Garden Pea Soup, to heavy
plates of food. These fancy finger foods
are also conveniently shared with her
many visitors.

DEVILS ON HORSEBACK

———— ❧❧ ————

These Stilton-stuffed dates are mysteriously called "Devils on Horseback," a name
that delights Lady Danbury, who has a wicked sense of humor. Another favorite at
Danbury gambling parties, these perfect savory treats are meant to be grasped with
two fingers and relished in a moment, between hands.

Makes 24 total

4 ounces cream cheese, at room temperature	¼ cup smoked almonds, finely chopped	6 slices bacon, cut into ½-inch pieces
2 ounces Stilton cheese, crumbled (about ½ cup)	Freshly ground black pepper	24 pitted large Medjool dates (about 1 pound)
	2 teaspoons vegetable oil	Microgreens, for serving

1. In a medium bowl, combine the cream cheese, Stilton, smoked almonds, and
several large grinds of black pepper. Stir until well combined, cover, and chill in the
refrigerator while you cook the bacon.

2. Line a large plate with paper towels.

3. In a medium skillet over medium heat, warm the vegetable oil. Add the bacon and
cook, stirring occasionally, until the fat has rendered and the bacon is crisp, about
15 to 20 minutes. Transfer to the paper towel–lined plate to drain. Set aside the
skillet with the rendered fat; this will be used to brush on the dates.

4. Preheat the oven to 375°F. Line a baking sheet with parchment.

5. Working with one date at a time, locate the incision on the side of the date where
the pit was removed and use a small paring knife to lengthen it so that it goes from
the top to the bottom of the date. Use your fingers to squeeze open the date, then
stuff it with a heaping teaspoon of the chilled filling. Use the back of a small spoon
to lightly press down on the filling, then use your fingers to bring the date up and
around the filling so it is a compact package. Transfer the stuffed date to the baking
sheet. Repeat with the remaining dates and filling.

6. Brush the stuffed dates with a light coating of the rendered bacon fat (heat the fat
briefly if it has hardened), then roast in the oven until the dates and filling are hot
throughout, about 10 minutes. Cool the dates on the baking sheet for 10 minutes.

7. Scatter a handful of microgreens on a platter. Finely chop the bacon pieces.
Transfer the dates to the platter, sprinkle the dates with the bacon bits, and serve.

———— ❦ ————

CHILLED ENGLISH GARDEN PEA SOUP

In Georgian England, the working class sustained themselves by consuming a hearty pea soup made from dried peas, while the upper class savored a more refined variation made from harvested fresh garden peas. Lady Danbury enjoys a lighter, chilled alternative, which she serves at a seasonable summer party in her London garden.

Makes 8 to 12 servings

3 tablespoons extra-virgin olive oil, plus additional for drizzling

1 large shallot, coarsely chopped

Kosher salt and freshly ground black pepper

2 garlic cloves, minced

12 ounces shelled fresh English peas (about 2½ cups)

1 cup vegetable stock

½ cup cold water, plus additional as needed

1 tablespoon chopped fresh tarragon

2 tablespoons chopped fresh dill, plus additional hand-torn dill, for topping

Pinch of ground white pepper

Hand-torn pea tendrils, for garnish (optional)

1. In a skillet over medium heat, warm 2 tablespoons of the olive oil until it starts to shimmer. Add the shallot and a pinch of salt and black pepper and cook, stirring occasionally, until tender, 6 to 8 minutes. Add the garlic and cook, stirring constantly, until softened, 2 to 3 minutes. Transfer the mixture to a bowl and let cool.

2. Fill a medium bowl with ice water and season the water aggressively with salt.

3. Fill a large saucepan with water and bring to a boil over medium heat. Season it aggressively with salt and add the peas. Cook until the peas turn bright green and are tender but not mushy, about 1 minute. Strain the English peas, transfer in the strainer to the ice bath, and stir several times until the peas are no longer hot.

4. Place the chilled peas in a blender along with the shallot and garlic mixture, the remaining tablespoon of olive oil, the stock, ½ cup cold water, the tarragon, 2 tablespoons dill, a large pinch of salt, and the white pepper. Puree until smooth; the soup should be thick but pourable. Adjust the consistency with water, if needed.

5. Chill the soup in the refrigerator for at least 1 hour and up to overnight.

6. To serve, taste the soup and adjust the seasoning with more salt and white pepper, if needed, then divide the chilled soup among shooter glasses or other small cups. Drizzle with more olive oil, then garnish with additional dill and the pea tendrils (if using).

BRITISH SAUSAGE ROLLS

Mini sausage rolls represent the quintessential comfort snack. They are a popular addition to a picnic spread but also great as an appetizer or a late-night snack at a gambling party in the Danbury Den of Iniquity. Alternatively, you could make larger rolls and serve them with a salad for lunch. Sausage rolls are particularly gratifying when prepared from scratch, but using store-bought puff pastry is by no means a crime. Resourceful cooks prepare these sausage rolls in advance and freeze them for those moments when they crave a savory indulgence or require a delightful appetizer for anticipated guests.

Makes 24 total

1 tablespoon canola oil

½ small yellow onion, finely diced (about 1 cup)

Kosher salt and freshly ground black pepper

2 teaspoons coarsely chopped fresh thyme

6 large fresh sage leaves, coarsely chopped (about 2 teaspoons)

1 pound ground pork

1½ teaspoons dry mustard

1¼ teaspoons granulated garlic

½ teaspoon freshly grated nutmeg

2 tablespoons cold water

2 teaspoons Worcestershire sauce

1 large egg

All-purpose flour, for dusting

2 sheets frozen puff pastry (from one 17.3-ounce package, such as Pepperidge Farm), thawed

Flaky sea salt, for topping

English mustard, for serving

1. In a medium skillet over medium heat, warm the oil until it starts to shimmer. Add the onion and a small pinch of kosher salt and pepper and cook, stirring occasionally, until tender, about 10 minutes. Turn off the heat, stir in the thyme and sage, and transfer to a large bowl. Set aside to cool completely.

2. Once cooled, add the pork, mustard, granulated garlic, nutmeg, 1¾ teaspoons kosher salt, several large grinds of pepper, the water, and Worcestershire sauce to the onions. Use your hands to mix until well combined, then cover and chill in the refrigerator for at least 30 minutes and up to overnight.

3. Line a baking sheet with parchment. In a small bowl, whisk together the egg and a small splash of water.

4. Lightly dust a clean work surface with flour, then top with one of the puff pastry sheets. Unfold the puff pastry, and use a rolling pin to roll it into a 9 by 10-inch rectangle. Cut the sheet in half lengthwise to make two 4½ by 10-inch strips.

recipe continues

5. Divide the sausage mixture into 4 portions. Using damp hands and a bench scraper, if needed, roll 2 portions into 10-inch logs (about 1 inch thick), then lay a sausage log lengthwise in the middle of each pastry rectangle.

6. Brush any of the exposed pastry with the egg wash. Roll the top and bottom sides of the pastry over the sausage to meet and slightly overlap in the middle. Carefully pinch to seal the seam, then use your hands to gently press the pastry against the sausage so it pushes out any air and creates a compact log. Turn the logs so they are seam side down, then transfer to the baking sheet. Repeat the process with the remaining puff pastry and sausage mixture to create 4 sausage logs. Chill the logs in the refrigerator until the puff pastry is firm, about 30 minutes.

7. Preheat the oven to 400°F.

8. Use a serrated knife to cut each log crosswise into 6 pieces (about 1½ inches long). Arrange the cut sausage rolls seam side down on the baking sheet, spacing them about 1 inch apart.

9. Brush the tops and sides of the pastry on each sausage roll with the remaining egg wash, then top with a light sprinkle of flaky sea salt and coarsely ground black pepper. Bake until the pastry is puffed and golden brown and the sausage is firm to the touch, about 25 minutes, rotating the baking sheet once after 15 minutes.

10. Cool the sausage rolls on the baking sheet for 10 minutes, then transfer to a serving platter and serve warm with English mustard on the side.

PÂTE *de* FRUITS

"The first ball is no small thing. I do not take it lightly."
—LADY DANBURY

The flavors of these fruity candies marry the separate strands of Lady Danbury's early and adult life. Guava represents her childhood in Sierra Leone, while raspberry embodies her decades-long life in London. Imagine these pâte de fruits as part of a decadent spread of sweet offerings at one of Lady Danbury's most elegant balls. An early form of candy, pâte de fruits complement brandy, whisky, and any other cocktail or mocktail perfectly.

Makes about 80 pieces

FOR THE GUAVA PÂTE DE FRUITS

Nonstick cooking spray

1 cup frozen and thawed guava puree or pulp

1⅔ cups sugar

Kosher salt

1 (3-ounce) packet liquid pectin

1½ teaspoons fresh lime juice

FOR THE RASPBERRY PÂTE DE FRUITS

Nonstick cooking spray

8 ounces fresh raspberries

1⅔ cups sugar

Kosher salt

1 (3-ounce) packet liquid pectin

1½ teaspoons fresh lemon juice

COOK'S NOTE: *If you make the pâte de fruits in advance or have leftovers, arrange the pieces in a single layer in an airtight container and store at room temperature away from direct sunlight for up to 1 week. If the pâte de fruits absorbs the sugar coating as it sits, toss the pieces in additional sugar before serving.*

1. FOR THE GUAVA PÂTE DE FRUITS: Line the bottom of a 9 by 5-inch loaf pan with parchment, then lightly spray with cooking spray.

2. In a 1½ to 2-quart heavy-bottomed saucepan over medium heat, combine the guava puree, 1⅓ cups of the sugar, and a small pinch of salt. Bring the mixture to a simmer, 10 to 20 minutes, stirring occasionally. Continue to simmer, stirring frequently and adjusting the heat as needed, until the mixture reaches 233°F on an instant-read thermometer, 50 to 75 additional minutes. Stir in the pectin and bring the mixture back to a strong simmer (this happens very quickly), then allow the mixture to simmer for 1 full minute, stirring constantly.

3. Working quickly, stir in the lime juice, then immediately pour the guava mixture into the loaf pan. Cool the pâte de fruits completely at room temperature, at least 4 hours and up to overnight. When set, sprinkle the top with 1 tablespoon of sugar

recipe continues

and shake it around in the loaf pan so the top is completely coated. Use a small offset spatula to loosen the sides of the pâte, then gently flip it out onto a cutting board. Remove the parchment and sprinkle the other side with 1 tablespoon of sugar.

4. Wipe out the loaf pan so that it is dry and no longer sticky, then pour the remaining sugar into the pan. Use a long, sharp knife to cut the pâte de fruits into ¾-inch squares, or use your favorite small cookie cutters to cut out fun shapes. In small batches, roll the cut pieces in the sugar in the loaf pan, then arrange in a single layer on a large platter and serve.

5. FOR THE RASPBERRY PÂTE DE FRUITS: Line the bottom of a 9 by 5-inch loaf pan with parchment, and lightly spray with cooking spray. Set a fine-mesh strainer over a 1½ to 2-quart heavy-bottomed saucepan.

6. In a blender, combine the raspberries, ⅓ cup of the sugar, and a small pinch of salt and blend until smooth. Pour the raspberry puree into the strainer and use the back of a spoon to push the puree through the strainer and into the saucepan. Discard the seeds and stir 1 cup of sugar into the raspberry puree. Place the saucepan on the stovetop and turn to medium heat. Bring the mixture to a simmer, 10 to 20 minutes, stirring occasionally. Continue to simmer, stirring frequently and adjusting the heat as needed, until the mixture reaches 238°F on an instant-read thermometer, 40 to 60 additional minutes. Stir in the pectin and bring the mixture back to a strong simmer (this happens very quickly), then simmer for 1 full minute, stirring constantly.

FRUIT JELLIES

Since the Middle Ages, fruit jellies have been a staple on the banquet tables of the nobility. They were an early form of candy known as "fruit cheese," or pâte de fruits, and were created by slowly cooking fruit and sugar until it condensed into a thick paste that could be cut or molded into attractive shapes. This process could take hours, which is why we provide a quicker version here using pectin. Pâte de fruits is still a fashionable and expensive sweet treat in France today.

7. Working quickly, stir in the lemon juice, then immediately pour the raspberry mixture into the loaf pan. Let cool completely at room temperature, at least 4 hours and up to overnight. When set, sprinkle the top with 1 tablespoon sugar and shake it around in the pan so the top is completely coated. Use a small offset spatula to loosen the sides, then gently flip the pâte out onto a cutting board. Remove the parchment, then sprinkle the other side with 1 tablespoon sugar.

8. Wipe out the loaf pan so it is dry and no longer sticky, then pour the remaining sugar into the pan. Use a long, sharp knife to cut the pâte de fruits into ¾-inch squares, or use your favorite small cookie cutters to cut out fun shapes. In small batches, roll the pieces in the sugar in the loaf pan, then arrange in a single layer on a large platter and serve.

ESTEEMED LADIES SALAD

Endive and Treviso Leaves with Quark Cheese and Pickled Mushrooms

Pickled mushrooms were incredibly popular during the Georgian period, and this recipe, inspired by a recipe in a ladies' recipe notebook, has been tried and tested over time. The esteemed Lady Danbury takes pleasure in a well-crafted salad on those rare evenings when her social calendar is free, relishing the delightful bursts of mushroom paired with the bitter salad greens and the herbed quark cheese of this particular dish. Through this salad, we can observe the transition from summer, with its bitter leaves, to autumn and its medley of mushrooms.

Makes 8 to 12 servings

2 clusters brown beech (shimeji) mushrooms (about 7 ounces)

1 (1-inch) piece fresh ginger

1 cup apple cider vinegar

¾ cup water

3 tablespoons sugar

Kosher salt and freshly ground black pepper

4 whole cloves

¼ teaspoon freshly grated nutmeg

1 teaspoon white or black peppercorns

1 dried bay leaf

1½ cups quark cheese

½ cup fresh mint leaves, coarsely chopped

½ cup (lightly packed) fresh flat-leaf parsley leaves, coarsely chopped

⅓ cup salted roasted peanuts, finely chopped

1 small garlic clove, finely grated

1 tablespoon finely grated lemon zest

1 tablespoon extra-virgin olive oil, plus additional for drizzling

2 large heads of endive, leaves separated (about 12)

1 small head of treviso, leaves separated and trimmed to 4 to 5 inches long, if needed (about 12)

COOK'S NOTE: *If quark cheese proves hard to source, you can use 1 cup thick ricotta mixed with ½ cup sour cream.*

1. Trim off the bases of the beech mushrooms, then use your hands to separate the mushrooms into individual pieces (the teeny-tiny ones can stay in small clusters), and transfer to a large heatproof 1-quart glass jar.

2. Peel the ginger and cut it in half. Use the back side of a large knife to lightly smash down on the ginger several times, then place it in a small saucepan. Add the vinegar, water, sugar, 1 tablespoon salt, the cloves, nutmeg, peppercorns, and bay leaf. Turn the heat to medium and warm it until the mixture comes to a simmer, about 3 minutes, stirring occasionally. Remove from the heat, let cool for 10 minutes, then

recipe continues

pour the pickling brine over the mushrooms in the jar, lightly pressing down on the mushrooms to cover with the brine. Cool completely at room temperature, then cover the jar with a lid and chill in the refrigerator for 24 hours and up to 2 weeks.

3. In a medium bowl, combine the quark cheese, mint, parsley, peanuts, garlic, lemon zest, 1 tablespoon olive oil, a large pinch of salt, and several grinds of black pepper. Stir to combine and season with more salt and pepper, if needed.

4. Spread heaping tablespoons of the herbed quark cheese onto the endive and treviso leaves. Use a fork to lift the mushrooms out of the brine and arrange on top of the cheese. Transfer the leaves to a large platter, drizzle with more olive oil, and serve.

POSH PLAINTAIN BREAD

"There is nothing more beautiful or more constant than change."
—LADY DANBURY

Like the Ginger Beer (page 116), this recipe for rice bread pays tribute to Lady Danbury's Sierra Leonean heritage. The cake bears a resemblance to sweet banana bread, but it's crafted using ripe plantains (though ripe bananas can serve as a substitute). Alongside rice and plantains, spices are incorporated to infuse a touch of warmth. These cakes are a delicious, yet substantial afternoon snack served with a cup of strong black tea or coffee, though we suspect Lady Danbury also likes them for breakfast, spread generously with butter.

Makes 8 mini loaves

½ cup vegetable oil, plus additional for greasing

2 pounds very ripe yellow plantains (3 to 4 large) or very ripe bananas (5 to 6 large)

⅓ to ½ cup sugar

Kosher salt

1¾ cups unsweetened white rice flour

¾ teaspoon baking soda

½ teaspoon baking powder

2 teaspoons freshly grated nutmeg

¾ teaspoon ground ginger

2 large eggs, at room temperature

½ cup whole milk, at room temperature

1 teaspoon distilled white vinegar or apple cider vinegar

SPECIAL EQUIPMENT: 1 (8-cup) mini loaf pan

COOK'S NOTE: *You can also bake the batter in one large 9 by 5-inch loaf pan. The baking time will increase to 60 to 80 minutes, and the pan should be rotated once after the first 40 minutes. Loosely cover with foil if at any time the bread starts to become too dark before it is cooked through. Cool the bread in the loaf pan for 15 minutes, then invert it onto a wire rack and cool completely before slicing and serving.*

1. Lightly grease the 8 cups of a mini loaf pan.

2. Peel and coarsely chop the plantains and transfer to a large bowl. (If the plantains are extremely ripe, just peel and hand-tear the fruit into chunks directly into the bowl.) Add ½ cup sugar and ½ teaspoon salt to the plantains (or ⅓ cup sugar, if using bananas). Set aside until the sugar has dissolved and coats the fruit in a sweet syrup, 20 to 30 minutes. This helps coax the natural sugars from the fruit and ensures the fruit softens nicely.

3. Spoon the plantain mixture into a food processor or blender and blend until smooth. Pour back into the bowl.

recipe continues

4. In a small bowl, whisk together the rice flour, baking soda, baking powder, nutmeg, and ginger.

5. Into the bowl with the plantains, add the eggs, milk, the ½ cup vegetable oil, and the vinegar, then whisk until smooth. Add the rice flour mixture and whisk again until smooth. Divide the batter among the cups in the loaf pan (about a scant ¾ cup each). Depending on the depth of the cups, the batter might come up to the top, but that is okay. Any leftover batter can be poured into a greased ramekin and baked alongside the loaves. Let the loaf pan sit while the oven preheats.

6. Preheat the oven to 350°F.

7. Place the loaf pan in the oven and bake until the loaves are puffed, lightly browned on top, and a wooden skewer or cake tester inserted into the center of one of them comes out clean (a few moist crumbs are fine, but it should not have any wet batter on it), 30 to 40 minutes, rotating the pan once after 20 minutes. If you baked extra batter in a ramekin, check it after 20 minutes. Let the loaves cool in the pan for 10 minutes, then use a small offset spatula or butter knife to loosen the sides and carefully flip the breads out onto a rack to cool completely.

HOMEMADE SIERRA LEONE–STYLE GINGER BEER

Fresh ginger, cloves, lime juice, and a touch of sugar make for a robust, refreshing, and slightly spicy ginger beer. Even though it was invented in England in the mid-eighteenth century, ginger beer is a staple drink in Sierra Leone. A perfect drink for a garden soirée or picnic, it also makes an excellent alcohol-free substitute for cocktails or punches at a ball. In her schemes and strategic matchmaking for her protégées, Lady Danbury avoids the spirited allure of alcoholic tipples. After all, navigating the intricate currents of the marriage mart is akin to sailing on treacherous waters, and maintaining a sharp mind is of utmost importance.

Makes 6 to 8 servings, about 1½ cups

1 (8-ounce) piece fresh ginger, peeled and coarsely chopped (about 2 cups)	10 cups water	6 whole cloves
	¾ to 1 cup sugar	Lime slices, for garnish (optional)
	⅓ to ½ cup fresh lime juice	

1. In a blender, combine the ginger and ¾ cup of the water and blend until the mixture forms a smooth, thick paste.

2. Place a large fine-mesh strainer over a large bowl and wet several layers of cheesecloth, then drape the cheesecloth over the strainer. Pour the ginger paste into the strainer.

3. Add 1¼ cups of the water to the blender and blend to pick up any remaining ginger in the bowl, then slowly pour the ginger liquid over the ginger paste. Allow the water to gradually drip through the strainer. Slowly pour the remaining 8 cups water, 1 to 2 cups a time, through the ginger paste until all the water has been added. Gather the cheesecloth over the strainer and squeeze out any remaining juices into the bowl.

4. Add ¾ cup sugar, ⅓ cup lime juice, and the cloves and stir until the sugar is dissolved. Taste and adjust with additional sugar and/or lime juice. Cover and chill in the refrigerator for at least 2 hours and up to overnight.

5. When ready to serve, use a slotted spoon to remove the cloves and pour the ginger beer into serving glasses filled with ice. Garnish with the lime slices (if using) and serve. (If the ginger sediment settles to the bottom of the bowl, just give it a good stir to combine everything again.) Any leftover ginger beer can be stored in the refrigerator for up to 7 days.

PORT COCKTAILS
Two Ways

———— ❈ ————

After realizing that she didn't like drinking straight port, a young Lady Danbury found herself with a cellar filled with bottles of it. Establishing herself as the true Lady of the house, she instructed her staff to come up with two clever ways to use port in a cocktail that she would enjoy. Now she serves these port cocktails in her Den of Iniquity.

The Summer White Port and Tonic showcases cherries, the ruby-red gems of summer, while the Winter Hot Port Toddy gives warmth on colder days, with a pleasing mixture of sweet honey and the citrus notes of orange and lemon, all finished with a touch of cinnamon.

Makes 1 cocktail

SUMMER WHITE PORT AND TONIC

6 sour or sweet cherries, stemmed and pitted

Ice cubes, as needed

½ cup tonic water

¼ cup (2 ounces) white port wine

Lemon twist, for garnish

WINTER HOT PORT TODDY

1 (¼-inch-thick) half-moon slice of orange

3 whole cloves

1 to 2 teaspoons honey

1 teaspoon fresh lemon juice

½ cup (4 ounces) ruby port wine

½ cup water

1 cinnamon stick

THE HOT TODDY

As is the case with many foods and drinks in history, the origin of the toddy is shrouded in uncertainty and often is associated with colonialism. In the seventeenth century, a Hindi beverage known as a *taddy* was crafted from fermented palm sap. It is plausible that, during their occupation of India in the eighteenth century, the British encountered this drink and brought it back to Britain. In 1788, a book titled *Grose Classical Dictionary of the Vulgar Tongue* mentioned the toddy as originally the juice of the cacao tree, and later a concoction of rum, water, sugar, and nutmeg. Initially served cold, the toddy evolved into an exclusively hot drink. Hot toddies are versatile and open to various interpretations and adjustments.

1. FOR THE SUMMER DRINK: Put the cherries in a highball glass and muddle to release the juices. Fill the glass with ice cubes, then pour in the tonic water followed by the white port. Stir lightly, garnish with the lemon twist, and serve.

2. FOR THE WINTER DRINK: Stud the peel of the orange slice with the cloves. In a large heat-safe mug, combine the honey and lemon juice. In a small saucepan over medium heat, combine the ruby port, water, and cinnamon stick. Stir together, then warm over medium heat until the mixture is hot and steamy, about 2 minutes. Carefully pour the warm port (along with the cinnamon stick) into the mug and give the toddy a good stir. Place the clove-studded orange slice directly into the drink and serve.

STEAMED LEMON PUDDINGS

Typically served as individual puddings, in period cookery books these puddings are often referred to as "castle puddings," perhaps because they resemble castle battlements when arranged in a circle on a plate. The puddings come out as the moistest sponge cakes ever tasted, an advantage of steaming rather than baking cake batter.

Makes 6 servings

10 tablespoons (1¼ sticks) unsalted butter, at room temperature, plus additional for greasing

⅔ cup sugar

1 tablespoon finely grated lemon zest

3 large eggs, at room temperature

1 cup self-rising flour

2 tablespoons lemon juice

¼ cup jarred lemon curd

Clotted cream or whipped cream, for serving

Mixed fresh berries and mint, for garnish

SPECIAL EQUIPMENT:
6 (6-ounce) pudding basins or ramekins with sloped sides

COOK'S NOTE: *Regency cooks had to make these puddings à la minute, but fortunately we live in a world where we can steam the puddings in advance and simply heat them in the microwave just before serving. If you don't have traditional English pudding basins, a sturdy teacup is an excellent vessel for steaming the puddings to get the iconic shape. A deep muffin tin works just fine as well. If you use ramekins instead of pudding basins, the puddings may bake differently and the lemon curd may cook into the cake rather than sit on top when turned out. If this is the case, add a dollop of lemon curd on top just before serving.*

1. Preheat the oven to 350°F. Lightly grease 6 (6-ounce) pudding basins or sloped ramekins with a light coating of butter. Cut a disk of parchment to fit in the bottom of each basin and press it into the butter. Grease the parchment with more butter.

2. Fill a large saucepan with water and place over medium heat to warm while you make the batter.

3. In a large bowl, use an electric hand mixer on medium-high speed to beat the 10 tablespoons butter, the sugar, and lemon zest until light and fluffy, about 2 minutes. Reduce the speed to low and beat in the eggs, one at a time, stopping and scraping down the bowl occasionally. Add a heaping tablespoon of the flour along with the last egg to prevent the batter from curdling. Add half the flour and blend on low speed until the batter is almost combined (a few streaks of flour is fine). Add the lemon juice and blend until almost smooth, then add the remaining flour and blend until smooth.

recipe continues

4. Spoon 2 teaspoons of the lemon curd into each pudding basin, then divide the batter evenly among the basins. Transfer the basins to a large roasting pan and pour the hot water into the pan until it comes a little less than halfway up the sides of the basins. Cover the pan with aluminum foil and bake until the cakes have puffed and a cake tester or wooden skewer inserted into the one of the center puddings comes out clean (do not poke it all the way to the bottom, where the curd is), 40 to 55 minutes, checking the puddings at the 40-minute mark. Cool the puddings in the roasting pan for 10 minutes, then transfer the basins to a wire rack and cool completely.

5. To serve, loosen the puddings from the basins with a butter knife or small offset spatula, and turn the puddings out onto 6 individual serving plates. Remove the parchment from each pudding. Serve with a dollop of clotted cream or whipped cream and garnish with fresh berries.

MINI BUBBLE AND SQUEAK

———————— ✦ ————————

The kitchen staff at Danbury House creates this dish using leftovers from the dinner
table. Cooking just for Lady Danbury means lots of leftovers; as it would not be proper
for a lady to eat the same dish twice, the cook puts these leftovers to good use for staff
meals. Traditionally, bubble and squeak was prepared using cabbage and any other
leftover vegetables and cooked meat from dinners past. The name is derived from
the sound that cabbage makes when it is added to a hot pan, producing bubbles and
squeaks, as the cook chops the vegetables and meat into smaller pieces while frying.
These mini bubble and squeaks make a perfect breakfast or brunch dish.
While eggs were not originally included, they have become a common
addition, usually replacing the leftover meat.

Makes 6 to 8 servings

1½ pounds russet potatoes
(about 3 medium)

Kosher salt

8 ounces fresh green or savoy
cabbage, cut into ½-inch pieces
(about 1½ cups)

2 tablespoons unsalted butter, at
room temperature

2 tablespoons heavy cream

Freshly ground black pepper

1½ cups coarsely chopped
roasted vegetables

1 large egg, beaten

1⅓ cups all-purpose flour, plus
additional for dusting

Grapeseed oil, for pan-frying

Sliced fresh chives, scallions, or
spring onion greens, for garnish

1. Put the potatoes in a large saucepan and add enough water to cover by 1 inch.
Bring to a boil over medium-high heat, about 15 minutes. Stir in a generous amount
of salt and cook until the potatoes are fork-tender, about 20 minutes. Use a large
slotted spoon to remove the potatoes from the water and set aside to cool slightly.

2. Bring the water back to a boil, add the cabbage, and cook until crisp-tender, about
2 minutes. Drain well.

3. Peel the potatoes and place in a medium bowl. Add the butter, cream, a large
pinch of salt, and several large grinds of pepper and mash well (it doesn't have to be
super smooth; a few small lumps are fine). Add the cabbage and the vegetables and
stir until well combined. Taste and season with additional salt and pepper, as needed.

4. Add the egg and ⅓ cup of the flour to the bowl and mix well. Cover the bowl and
transfer to the refrigerator to chill, at least 1 hour and up to overnight.

recipe continues

———————— ✦ ————————

5. Preheat the oven to 250°F. Set a wire rack on top of a baking sheet and generously dust a second large baking sheet with flour.

6. Scoop the potato mixture into 16 equal mounds (about ⅓ cup each) and place the mounds on the floured baking sheet. With damp hands, shape each mound into a patty a little more than ½ inch thick and about 2½ inches in diameter.

7. Spread the remaining 1 cup flour on a wide plate and season with salt. Pour enough grapeseed oil into a large cast-iron skillet to cover the bottom of the skillet by a scant ⅛ inch. Place the skillet on medium-high heat; the oil is hot enough when you sprinkle a bit of flour into the oil and it sizzles immediately.

8. Dredge 4 of the patties in the seasoned flour, then add to the hot oil. Cook until deeply golden brown and crisp on the first side, 3 to 5 minutes. Use 2 spatulas to carefully flip over each patty (careful, they will be delicate) and cook until browned and crisp on the other side, 3 to 5 additional minutes. Transfer the patties to the wire rack and place in the warm oven. Repeat, cooking the remaining patties and placing in the oven as they are finished.

9. Arrange the mini bubble and squeaks on a serving platter, garnish with the chives, scallions, or spring onion greens, and serve.

❖

LADY DANBURY

The DUKE *and* DUCHESS *of* HASTINGS

"Just because something is not perfect does not make it any less worthy of love."
—DAPHNE BRIDGERTON

The Duke and Duchess of Hastings caused quite a stir in London society when they were courting. Even though Simon and Daphne's relationship started as a scheme to find her a suitable match, they fell deeply in love while playing their games. Now that this beloved couple is happily wed, the romance continues with intimate dinners, like the Artichokes for Two, and grander dishes, like the Impressive Game Pie. Of course, there is also the Duke's favorite Gooseberry Pie and some delightfully sensual ice cream.

  The besotted Simon welcomes Daphne's changes to the Hastings kitchen, where she introduces some of the classic English fare Daphne enjoyed at her paternal home and some showstopping dishes the Bridgertons were known for at their dinner parties. With her presence, she transforms the Hastings world into a true home for Simon, instilling a warmth and constancy. The future Hastings brood will flourish in this loving atmosphere, where they will undoubtedly enjoy many family moments around a well-set table.

IMPRESSIVE GAME PIE

───────────❀───────────

This standing game pie is an absolute showstopper, its grandeur making it perfect for Christmas and other big celebrations. Freestanding pies were highly fashionable in the Georgian period; the more intricate the crust decoration, the greater the praise it would garner from guests. Members of the ton competed for a cook with the exceptional pastry skills to make a showcase pie for dinner. Such elaborate pies were a privilege reserved for grandest houses because of the expensive ingredients and the precious copper molds often used to craft them. Nowadays, you can use a springform or cake pan for your pie and then employ your imagination to create decorations with leftover pastry.

Makes 10 to 12 servings

FOR THE FILLING

12 ounces thick-cut bacon, cut into ¼-inch pieces

12 garlic cloves, minced

8 sprigs of fresh thyme, leaves stripped and finely chopped (about 1 tablespoon)

4 sprigs of fresh rosemary, leaves stripped and finely chopped (about 2 tablespoons)

2 sprigs of fresh marjoram, leaves stripped and finely chopped (about 2 teaspoons)

1 tablespoon pink peppercorns, lightly crushed

1½ teaspoons freshly grated nutmeg

1½ teaspoons ground allspice

1 teaspoon freshly ground black pepper

½ cup (4 ounces) sweet sherry

2 pounds boneless, skinless chicken breasts and/or thighs

1 pound boneless, skinless pheasant meat

1½ pounds boneless pork shoulder

1 pound boneless venison tenderloin

Kosher salt

1 cup water

½ ounce dried porcini mushrooms, rinsed

FOR THE HOT WATER CRUST

4½ cups all-purpose flour, sifted, plus extra for dusting

2¼ cups bread flour, sifted

2 cups water

1 cup pork lard, at room temperature

4 teaspoons chicken bouillon paste

1 large egg, lightly beaten

FOR THE ASSEMBLY

1 cup roasted unsalted pistachios

1 cup dried barberries or cranberries

FOR THE ASPIC

¼ cup (½ stick) unsalted butter

1 medium yellow onion, thinly sliced

8 sprigs of fresh thyme, leaves stripped

¼ cup (2 ounces) sweet sherry

2 cups water

¾ cup veal demi-glace

6 allspice berries

2 tablespoons unflavored powdered gelatin (2 envelopes)

Kosher salt

SPECIAL EQUIPMENT:
1 (10-inch) springform pan with 2¾-inch high sides and 1 (1½-inch) round biscuit cutter

recipe continues

───────────❀───────────

1. MAKE THE FILLING: In a large skillet, add the bacon, garlic, thyme, rosemary, marjoram, pink peppercorns, nutmeg, allspice, and pepper. Turn the heat to medium-low and cook, stirring frequently, until the bacon renders its fat and is cooked but not yet crisp, 8 to 10 minutes. Turn off the heat, stir in the sherry, and scrape the pan with a wooden spoon to release any brown bits. Let the mixture cool to room temperature.

2. Cut the chicken and pheasant into 1-inch strips and transfer to a large bowl. Cut the pork into 1-inch cubes and the venison into 1-inch-thick medallions, and add both to the bowl. Season the meats with 2 tablespoons of salt and use your hands to mix well.

3. Add the bacon mixture to the bowl, scraping the pan to include any sherry or bacon fat in the pan. Use your hands to massage the ingredients into the meat until evenly coated, then cover the bowl and marinate the meat in the refrigerator for 3 to 4 hours.

4. Meanwhile, pour the water into a small saucepan and bring to a simmer. Remove from the heat and add the porcini. Cover with the lid and let steep for 15 minutes to rehydrate the mushrooms and infuse the water. Use a slotted spoon to transfer the mushrooms to a cutting board. When cool enough, use your hands to squeeze out any excess water. Coarsely chop the mushrooms and set aside.

5. Line a fine-mesh strainer with cheesecloth and set it over a small bowl. Strain the porcini liquid to remove any sediment. Let the liquid cool completely at room temperature, then cover and set aside to use later in the aspic.

6. MAKE THE CRUST: Line 2 baking sheets with parchment.

7. In a large bowl, whisk the flours together.

8. In a medium saucepan over medium heat, combine the water, lard, and bouillon. Bring the mixture to a simmer and stir until the lard melts and everything is well combined, about 5 minutes. Pour the lard-water mixture into the bowl of flour and use a wooden spoon to stir until a shaggy dough forms. Turn the dough out onto a clean piece of parchment and knead the dough until it holds together and is somewhat smooth, about 1 minute. (Do not add any flour to knead the dough; it is not needed.) Shape the dough into a ¾-inch-thick rectangle that is about 10 by 6 inches. Wrap in parchment and refrigerate the dough until completely chilled, about 2 hours.

9. When the dough is chilled, remove the parchment and cut off approximately one-third of the dough and set that aside; this will be for the top crust and decorations. Lightly dust a clean work surface and rolling pin with flour. Roll the remaining dough into a 13½-inch round that is ¼ inch thick. Wrap up any excess dough to use later.

10. Using the rolling pin, transfer the dough round to a 10-inch springform pan with 2¾-inch sides, centering the dough in the pan. Gently press the dough to the edges and up the sides of the pan. If folds form, use your fingers to press them smooth so the dough has an even thickness all around. If there are any tears in the dough, press a bit of the excess dough into the tear to patch it. Use kitchen shears or a paring knife to trim along the top edge of the dough, leaving a ½-inch overhang. If any part of the edge is short, use some of the trimming and press it into the dough to even out the overhang. (If you need additional dough to patch the bottom crust, pinch off some of the dough reserved for the top crust.) Place the pan in the refrigerator.

11. Lightly dust your work surface and rolling pin again with flour. Roll the reserved top dough into a round that is ¼ inch thick. Cut the dough into a 10½-inch round (reserve any excess dough for decorations). Use a 1½-inch round biscuit cutter to cut a hole in the center of the round; this will be the top vent. Place the top crust on one of the baking sheets and refrigerate.

12. Again dust your work surface and rolling pin with flour. Gather together any dough trimmings and roll out to a ¼-inch thickness. Use decorative cutters or a paring knife to cut out desired decorations for the top of the pie. Place these cutouts on the other baking sheet and refrigerate.

13. ASSEMBLE AND BAKE: Place a rack in the center of the oven and preheat the oven to 350°F.

14. Remove the dough-lined springform pan and the marinated meat from the refrigerator. First, add the chicken and pheasant in an even layer on the bottom of the pan. When filling the meat in the pan, make sure to nestle the pieces next to each other but do not press them down. Next, evenly sprinkle the barberries over the meat, making sure they are spread from edge to edge. Top the barberries with the venison medallions, again in an even layer. Sprinkle the pistachios over the venison, again from edge to edge, then top the pistachios with the cubed pork; it is okay if the pork is slightly mounded in the middle. Sprinkle the chopped porcini over the pork.

15. Remove the top crust from the refrigerator and carefully lay it on top of the filling, making sure the vent is in the center. Gently press the dough down so it sits directly on the top of the filling. Pinch the edges of the crust together to seal the pie.

recipe continues

CHRISTMAS PIE

This type of pie, making the most of the game season, was traditionally a staple during Christmas and was frequently sent as a gift. Members of the ton who resided in the countryside during the winter often sent such pies over great distances. Their pastry crusts were made several inches thick to withstand the rigors of the journey in a horse-drawn carriage. Owing to slow land travel and a lack of refrigeration, reports from the time indicate that these gifted pies often arrived as health hazards.

Christmas pies could take on epic proportions, encasing whole boned turkeys stuffed with boned geese, chickens, partridges, and pigeons, with additional game meat used as filler. This concept is reminiscent of the more recent American dish turducken. In an eighteenth-century recipe, darker rabbit meat was used to fill the spaces on either side of the turkey, playing up the different colors of the cooked meats. An 1807 recipe uses mincemeat, ensuring that the filling holds together better when sliced, and emphasizing that the decoration on top of the pie must take the form of a flower.

16. To make the chimney for the pie vent, roll any excess dough you still have to a ¼-inch thickness. To ensure you have straight edges, use a ruler to measure and cut a 1-inch wide and 2-inch-long strip. Use the beaten egg to paint the edge of the vent, then roll up the strip. Use this strip to create a chimney that is about 1 inch high around the vent. Trim any excess dough on the strip when the 2 edges meet and then pinch to seal the dough. Use the beaten egg to adhere any other decorations you cut for the pie. Brush the entire top with the remaining beaten egg.

17. Place the springform pan on a baking sheet and bake until the crust is deep golden brown, about 3 hours, rotating the baking sheet once after 1½ hours. If at any time the crust starts to get too dark, loosely tent the top of the pie with aluminum foil. Remove the pie from the oven and let cool slightly.

18. MAKE THE ASPIC: In a medium saucepan over medium-low heat, melt the butter. Add the onion and thyme and cook, stirring occasionally, until softened and golden brown, 13 to 15 minutes. Stir in the sherry, use a wooden spoon to scrape the browned bits from the pan, and cook until the sherry has almost evaporated, 2 to 3 minutes. Add 1½ cups water, the demi-glace, the strained porcini liquid, and the allspice and stir to combine. Increase the heat to medium-high and bring to a boil, about 5 minutes. Reduce the heat to medium-low and simmer, stirring occasionally, until the liquid reduces to 2 cups, about 25 minutes.

19. Set a fine-mesh strainer over a medium bowl.

20. Meanwhile, in a small bowl, stir together the remaining ½ cup water and the gelatin, and allow the gelatin to bloom, about 5 minutes.

21. Pour the reduced aspic mixture through the strainer, pushing on the onion to release its flavor. Season to taste with salt, then whisk in the bloomed gelatin and stir until dissolved.

22. Pour the aspic mixture into a pitcher or liquid measuring cup with a pour spout. Then very slowly pour the aspic, a little at a time, into the vent of the slightly cooled pie. This process can take around 15 minutes, as only a little aspic can be poured into the vent at a time. Use a skewer to poke down into the vent if the aspic is having a hard time settling into the pie. Occasionally tilt the pie to the left and right to ensure the aspic is spreading evenly through the pie. Allow the pie to cool completely at room temperature, then chill it in the refrigerator overnight to set the aspic.

23. The next day, unmold the pie from the springform pan and transfer to a serving platter. It can be served cold or can be set out for an hour to take the chill off slightly. Use a serrated knife to cut the pie into thick wedges.

SALMON *with* SHRIMP SAUCE

———— ❁ ————

This recipe is inspired by one published in 1757 in *The Cook's Paradise,* by William Verral, who served as the master cook at the White Horse Inn in Lewes, Sussex. When the newlyweds Daphne and Simon stopped at an inn on their way to the Hastings' estate, they might have come across just this kind of salmon dish on the menu. It has been seamlessly woven into the Hastings' dinner repertoire. This dish, adorned with the fragrant embrace of herbs and scallions, gains an additional savory dimension courtesy of the shrimp.

Makes 6 to 8 servings

1 cup (8 ounces) dry white wine

½ cup water

3½ tablespoons extra-virgin olive oil

1 (2½-pound) salmon fillet, preferably center cut, skin removed

Kosher salt and freshly ground black pepper

1 small shallot, sliced into thick rounds

6 sprigs of fresh flat-leaf parsley, leaves stripped and stems reserved

4 sprigs of fresh thyme

2 scallions, trimmed, white bottoms left whole and green tops thinly sliced

12 ounces large (21 to 25 per pound) shrimp, peeled and deveined

3 garlic cloves, minced

1 tablespoon fresh lemon juice

3 tablespoons unsalted butter, cold, cut into small cubes

Handful of torn fresh basil leaves, for topping

Lemon wedges, for serving

1. Preheat the oven to 275°F.

2. In a 9 by 13-inch baking dish, combine ½ cup white wine, the water, and 2 tablespoons of the olive oil. Season the salmon liberally on both sides with salt and pepper, then place the fish top side up in the baking dish. Scatter the shallot, parsley stems, thyme sprigs, and the scallion bottoms around the salmon, then spoon some of the poaching liquid over the top of the fish.

3. Cover the baking dish with aluminum foil and bake for 20 minutes. Remove the foil and spoon some of the poaching liquid over the fish. Cover again with the foil and cook until the fish is opaque, buttery, and an instant-read thermometer inserted into the thickest part of the salmon registers 125°F, checking every 10 minutes and spooning additional poaching liquid over the fish, about 20 additional minutes. (The timing for this will vary depending on the thickness of your fish.) Remove the foil and let the fish keep warm in the poaching liquid.

recipe continues

———— ❁ ————

4. In a large skillet set on medium to medium-high heat, warm the remaining 1½ tablespoons olive oil. Season the shrimp liberally with salt and pepper, then add to the skillet in a single layer. Cook until lightly browned and opaque, about 1 minute per side. Transfer the shrimp to a plate and then add the garlic to the skillet and cook for 1 minute, stirring constantly. Add the remaining ½ cup wine and the lemon juice and increase the heat to medium-high. Cook until the liquid reduces by half, about 5 minutes. Reduce the heat to low and gradually whisk in the butter, 1 to 2 cubes at a time, to make a creamy and emulsified sauce. Return the shrimp to the skillet, turn to coat in the sauce, and cook for 1 additional minute. Season with more salt and pepper, if needed.

5. Use 2 wide, flat spatulas to transfer the salmon to a large serving platter. Spoon the shrimp and sauce over the fish, then sprinkle the top with the parsley leaves, scallion greens, and basil. Serve immediately, with lemon wedges on the side.

BOOZY DUCK
with Red Wine and Dried Fruit

This recipe takes full advantage of the abundant supply of duck on the Hastings estate. The dried fruit, wine, and spices are flavors favored by Daphne and have been the hallmark of aristocratic cooking for centuries, as these ingredients demonstrate the Hastings household's capacity to afford precious spices and imported dried fruits. While acquiring a whole duck might be more challenging for those of us not residing on a countryside estate, duck legs are readily available and this recipe works equally well with whole chicken legs, pheasant, and rabbit.

Makes 4 servings

4 whole duck legs (about 2½ pounds), excess fat trimmed

Kosher salt and freshly ground black pepper

3 small shallots, quartered lengthwise

2 medium carrots, peeled and sliced diagonally into ½-inch pieces

4 garlic cloves, lightly crushed

3 tablespoons tomato paste

¼ teaspoon ground allspice

1½ cups (12 ounces) fruity red wine, such as Merlot or Pinot Noir

1¼ cups low-sodium chicken stock

2 cups (heaping) mixed pitted dried fruits, such as prunes, apricots, and halved figs

2 large sprigs of fresh thyme

2 long strips of orange peel

2 dried bay leaves

1. Preheat the oven to 325°F.

2. Use a wooden skewer to prick the skin on the duck legs all over, then season liberally on both sides with salt and pepper. Lay the duck legs skin side down in a Dutch oven or large pot, then turn the heat to medium. Slowly render the fat from under the skin until skin is golden brown and slightly crisp, about 20 minutes. Turn up the heat slightly, then turn the duck legs over and cook until the other sides are lightly browned, about 10 minutes. Transfer to a plate.

3. Reserve 2 tablespoons of duck fat in the Dutch oven, then pour off any excess (if desired, save the extra fat to use in other recipes). Add the shallots, carrots, and garlic, then season with salt and pepper and cook until the vegetables are crisp-tender, about 10 minutes.

recipe continues

4. Stir in the tomato paste and allspice and cook, stirring constantly, for 2 minutes. Add the wine and cook until the liquid is reduced by about half, about 10 minutes.

5. Stir in the chicken stock, dried fruits, thyme, orange peel, and bay leaves. Nestle the duck legs skin side up in the cooking liquid and bring to a strong simmer, about 5 minutes. Partially cover with the lid, then cook in the oven until the duck is fork-tender and the braising liquid is slightly thickened, about 1½ hours. Remove and discard the bay leaves. Rest for 10 minutes, then transfer to a large platter with a rim and serve. For a more rustic (but still beautiful) presentation, serve the dish directly in the Dutch oven.

ARTICHOKES FOR TWO
with Browned Butter, Sage, and Thyme Dip

———— ❋ ————

This artichoke dish is an ideal choice for a romantic dinner for two at Hastings. Whether for a formal feast or an intimate dinner for two, these roasted artichokes are the stars of the show, looking stunning on a plate. The tasty dip features a nutty browned butter with thyme and sage to bring warmth, making it ideal for dipping those artichoke leaves.

Makes 2 servings

1 small lemon

4 garlic cloves

2 large globe artichokes (about 1 pound each)

Kosher salt

1 tablespoon extra-virgin olive oil

2 tablespoons water

½ cup (1 stick) salted butter

Freshly ground black pepper

1 dried bay leaf

5 large fresh sage leaves, coarsely chopped (about 2 teaspoons)

1½ teaspoons coarsely chopped fresh thyme leaves

1. Preheat the oven to 425°F. Cut 2 large squares of heavy-duty foil (each square should be large enough to wrap a whole artichoke).

2. Finely grate 2 teaspoons of zest from the lemon into a small bowl. Cut the lemon in half crosswise, then cut one of the halves into wedges. Place the wedges in a small bowl and refrigerate to use later. Save the remaining lemon half to rub on the artichokes while you prep them. Finely grate 2 of the garlic cloves and add to the bowl with the lemon zest.

3. Use a serrated knife to trim off the top third of the sturdy leaves on each artichoke, then cut off any remaining stem from the bottoms. Rub the cut side of the lemon half on the exposed tops and stem ends of the artichokes. Use kitchen shears to trim away any pointy tips on the remaining artichoke leaves. Place one artichoke on each square of aluminum foil and use your fingers to open up the centers to expose the inner leaves a bit, then nestle a whole garlic clove in the center of each artichoke. Drizzle the olive oil evenly over the artichokes and sprinkle liberally with salt. Use your hands to rub the oil and salt onto the artichoke leaves. Drizzle 1 tablespoon of water onto each artichoke, then wrap each tightly with the foil.

recipe continues

4. Place the wrapped artichokes on a baking sheet and roast until a paring knife slides easily into the stem end and an inner leaf pulls out without any resistance, 40 to 50 minutes. Unwrap the artichokes and let them cool for 10 minutes.

5. In a medium saucepan over medium heat, melt the butter, stirring occasionally, 3 to 5 minutes. Add several large grinds of pepper and the bay leaf and continue to cook, stirring frequently, until light brown specks start to form and the butter smells nutty, 5 to 8 additional minutes. Turn off the heat, and add the sage, thyme, lemon zest, and grated garlic. Cook for 30 seconds in the residual heat. (Be careful during this step because the mixture will get quite foamy and might sputter.) Discard the bay leaf and season the butter with additional salt and pepper, if needed.

6. Divide the browned butter between 2 ramekins and place on 2 serving plates. Position the roasted artichokes and the lemon wedges next to the butter and serve immediately.

The HASTINGS' CHRISTMAS CAKE

This Hastings' Christmas cake is based on a British classic, Dundee cake, a light rendition of the traditional dark British fruitcake that is typically baked for weddings and Christmas. Dundee cake hails from the Scottish town of Dundee, where marmalade maker James Keiller ingeniously utilized surplus orange peel from their marmalade production to craft the first Dundee cake. This cake traditionally features a lovely almond decoration on top and is made from a batter consisting of plain and almond flour, raisins, candied cherries, and candied orange peel. However, Daphne and Simon prefer orange marmalade and dried cranberries in their fruitcake, creating a more complex flavor. Cheese enthusiasts often savor a thin slice of this cake with their after-dinner cheese.

Makes 8 to 12 servings

½ cup (1 stick) plus 3 tablespoons unsalted butter, at room temperature, plus additional for greasing

1⅔ cups all-purpose flour

¼ cup superfine almond flour

1 teaspoon baking powder

¾ cup plus 1 tablespoon (packed) light brown sugar

Kosher salt

3 large eggs, at room temperature

⅓ cup good-quality chunky orange marmalade

1 tablespoon cream sherry

⅔ cup raisins

⅔ cup dried cranberries

½ cup whole blanched almonds, for topping

1 tablespoon hot water

SPECIAL EQUIPMENT:
1 (8-inch) springform pan

COOK'S NOTE: *If you cannot find whole blanched almonds at the grocery store, it is easy to do that yourself. Put the whole, raw, skin-on almonds into a bowl and top with boiling water. Let sit for exactly 1 minute (no more or else the almonds will start to cook and soften), then drain and rinse thoroughly with cold water until the almonds are chilled. Scatter the almonds on a clean kitchen towel and let sit until the skins start to shrivel, about 5 minutes. Use your fingers to tear the skin on a corner of each almond, pop the nuts out of their skins, and there you have it—blanched almonds!*

The cake can be stored for up to 1 week in an airtight container and is best prepared a day before consumption for the optimal experience.

1. Place a rack on the lowest shelf of the oven and preheat the oven to 350°F. Generously grease an 8-inch springform pan with butter, line the bottom with a round of parchment, and butter the parchment.

2. In a medium bowl, whisk together the all-purpose and almond flours and the baking powder.

recipe continues

3. In a large bowl, use an electric hand mixer set on medium-high speed to beat ½ cup of the butter, ¾ cup of the brown sugar, and ½ teaspoon salt until light and fluffy, about 3 minutes. Reduce the speed to low and beat in the eggs, one at a time, stopping and scraping down the bowl occasionally. Add 1 tablespoon of the flour mixture along with the last egg to prevent the batter from curdling.

4. Switch to a rubber spatula and gently stir in half the remaining flour mixture until almost combined (there can still be some streaks of flour). Add the orange marmalade, sherry, and the remaining flour mixture, then stir until smooth. Fold in the raisins and cranberries, then spoon the batter into the springform pan and smooth the top.

5. Lightly place the blanched almonds on top of the cake, arranging them in concentric circles. (Do not press the almonds into the batter or they might sink into the cake as it bakes.) Depending on the design you make, you might have leftover almonds.

6. Reduce the oven temperature to 300°F, place the cake on the lowest rack, and bake until the top and edges are golden brown and a cake tester or toothpick inserted into the center comes out clean, 70 to 90 minutes, rotating the pan once after 40 minutes. If the top of the cake starts to become too brown before the cake is finished baking, loosely cover the top with aluminum foil and continue baking as needed.

7. Meanwhile, in a small bowl, combine the remaining 1 tablespoon brown sugar and the hot water and stir until the sugar is completely dissolved.

8. Transfer the cake (still in its pan) to a wire rack and brush the top with the brown sugar syrup. Cool the cake completely in the pan, them remove before slicing and serving.

The DUKE OF HASTINGS'S GOOSEBERRY PIE

At the opera, we observe Lady Danbury and Lady Bridgerton conspiring about the Duke of Hastings attending his first dinner at the Bridgerton house. Lady Danbury inadvertently mentions one of Simon's favorite sweets, likely a treat he enjoyed during his childhood at Danbury House, when Lady Danbury was his guardian. This gooseberry pie is symbolic of his childhood and later life, with the fruit starting as tart green berries and transforming into a sweet jam when cooked into the pie.

Makes 8 to 10 servings

FOR THE PIE DOUGH

2¾ cups all-purpose flour, sifted, plus extra for dusting

½ teaspoon grated nutmeg (optional)

Kosher salt

1 cup (2 sticks) unsalted butter, cold

¼ cup ice water

1 large egg, lightly beaten

FOR THE GOOSEBERRY FILLING

4 pounds fresh gooseberries, any remaining blossoms removed, or goldenberries

2 cups sugar

¼ cup (2 ounces) orange liqueur, such as Grand Marnier

½ teaspoon freshly grated nutmeg

Kosher salt

½ cup (1 stick) unsalted butter

3 tablespoons cornstarch

COOK'S NOTES: *Gooseberries are large, tart berries often grown in northern Europe. They come in many varieties, including green, white, yellow, and red, and any variety will work for this recipe. They generally are in season during early summer. A great alternative to fresh gooseberries is fresh goldenberries (also known as cape gooseberries). While these fruits are similar in shape and both have tart yet sweet flavors, they are not related. The goldenberry is in the nightshade family, related to the tomatillo. If you use them here, rinse them thoroughly, as they have a similar sticky outside.*

1. MAKE THE PIE DOUGH: In a food processor, add the flour, nutmeg (if using), and 1 teaspoon salt and pulse to combine. Add the butter and pulse again until the ingredients resemble grated parmesan. With the food processor running, stream in the water, 1 tablespoon at a time, until the dough just comes together in a loose ball. You may not need all the water; the dough should be moist, but not wet.

2. Spread a large sheet of plastic wrap on a work surface. Turn the dough out onto the plastic wrap and form into a 1-inch-thick disk. Wrap the dough and chill in the refrigerator until firm, about 2 hours or up to overnight.

recipe continues

THE DUKE AND DUCHESS OF HASTINGS

3. MAKE THE FILLING: In a medium saucepan over medium-low heat, add the gooseberries, sugar, orange liqueur, nutmeg, and ¼ teaspoon salt. Stir the mixture several times as it heats up to help the sugar dissolve. Continue to cook, without stirring to avoid crushing the berries, until the berries soften and just begin to burst, about 15 minutes.

4. Place a strainer over a large bowl and pour in the hot gooseberry mixture. Allow the liquid to drain into the bowl, without pressing on the berries. Transfer the gooseberry mixture to a medium bowl and place in the refrigerator to chill. Reserve ½ cup of the juice and let cool at room temperature.

5. Pour the remaining juice into the saucepan and add the butter. Bring to a simmer over medium heat, and continue to simmer, stirring occasionally, until it has the consistency of maple syrup and coats the back of a spoon, about 30 minutes.

6. Whisk the cornstarch into the reserved ½ cup juice, then whisk it into the simmering syrup. Continue to simmer, stirring occasionally, until the sauce has thickened to the consistency of honey and has a sweet burnt-orange flavor, about 30 minutes. Pour the sauce onto the chilled berries and refrigerate again until completely chilled, about 2 hours.

7. ASSEMBLE AND BAKE: Preheat the oven to 375°F. Line 2 baking sheets with parchment.

8. Remove the chilled dough from the refrigerator and let sit at room temperature for 10 minutes. Lightly dust a rolling pin and a work surface with flour. Divide the dough in half. Roll each half into a 13-inch round that is ⅛ inch thick (reserve excess dough).

9. Put one dough round on one of the baking sheets and place in the refrigerator. Line a 10-inch glass or ceramic pie plate with the other dough round, pressing it gently into the edges and up the sides of the plate. Trim any excess dough at the edge with a paring knife and add to the rest of the excess dough. (Cover the excess dough with plastic wrap and refrigerate; this will be used for decorations later.) Gently crimp the edges of the pie crust and poke the bottom with a fork. Line the dough with parchment and fill with pie weights or dried beans. Bake until the edges of the crust are golden and set, about 25 minutes.

10. Remove the crust from the oven and reduce the oven temperature to 350°F. Remove the pie weights and parchment, and continue to bake the crust until the bottom is lightly golden, 10 to 15 additional minutes. Remove the parbaked crust from the oven and let cool to room temperature, about 30 minutes.

11. Remove the reserved excess dough from the refrigerator. Lightly dust your work surface and rolling pin with flour, then re-roll the dough until ⅛ inch thick. Use decorative cookie cutters or a paring knife to cut out decorations for the top crust and place on the second baking sheet.

12. Spoon the chilled filling into the pie crust. Remove the remaining dough round from the refrigerator and lay it on top of the filling, making sure it's centered. Crimp the edge of the top crust, making sure the top crust covers the rim of the bottom crust completely; the top crust will sit atop the bottom crust similar to a lid on a pot. Use a paring knife to cut several slits as vents in the top, then use the beaten egg to adhere the cut-out decorations to the top. Brush the entire top of the pie with more beaten egg.

13. Place the pie on a baking sheet and bake until the top crust is a deep golden brown and the filling is bubbly and thickened a touch more, about 1 hour 30 minutes. Remove from the oven and allow the pie to cool completely on a wire rack before slicing and serving. The pie is delicious at room temperature, but is even better served slightly chilled.

REGENCY PIE

Fruit pies in the Regency era took on various appearances. Typically baked in a shallow pie dish resembling a deep plate, they could feature a richly decorated pastry lid, pastry strips covering the fruit, or an open top to fully display the fruit filling. The finest short-crust pastry was used, often enhanced with a dash of freshly grated nutmeg, which was considered posh during the Regency era, to add a touch of spice.

LAVENDER PETTICOAT TAILS

A cup of English tea without a biscuit is unimaginable. Daphne, ever the traditionalist, adores these classic shortbread biscuits. They are versatile—delightful when enjoyed plain, but even more luxurious when enhanced with caraway seeds, lemon zest, and candied citrus peel, all of which were fashionable during the Georgian period. In this Bridgerton version, we've introduced lavender in the shortbread, topped with white lavender icing studded with edible flowers to add a nice touch of color.

Makes 8 to 12 biscuits

1 cup all-purpose flour, plus additional for dusting

2 tablespoons cornstarch

½ cup (1 stick) unsalted butter, at room temperature

1¼ cups confectioners' sugar

1 tablespoon culinary-grade lavender buds, finely chopped

Kosher salt

3 tablespoons milk

Edible flowers, for topping

SPECIAL EQUIPMENT:
1 (8-inch) fluted tart pan with removable bottom

PETTICOAT TAILS

Traditionally, these biscuits were made in a large, shallow, round mold imprinted with a pattern. Without a mold, they are made either as finger biscuits or as a large roundel decorated with a fork or stamp. When cut into segments, these biscuits are referred to as "petticoat tails."

1. In a medium bowl, whisk together the flour and cornstarch. In a large bowl, use an electric hand mixer set on medium-high speed to beat together the butter, ¼ cup of the confectioners' sugar, half the chopped lavender buds, and a small pinch of salt until smooth and lightly fluffy, about 2 minutes. Add half the flour mixture and mix just until almost combined. Add the remaining flour mixture and mix until a smooth dough forms.

2. Pat the dough evenly into the bottom of an 8-inch fluted tart pan with a removable bottom. Use a fork to prick the dough all over about 1 inch apart. Chill in the refrigerator for about 15 minutes.

3. Preheat the oven to 325°F.

4. Place the tart pan on a baking sheet, then bake until the shortbread is set and the edges are starting to brown, about 30 minutes, rotating the pan once after

recipe continues

15 minutes. Cool on a wire rack for 10 minutes, then remove the ring but keep the bottom still attached. Use a serrated knife to cut the warm shortbread into 8 to 12 wedges—or petticoat tails—and cool completely.

5. Meanwhile, in a small bowl, warm the milk in the microwave until hot and steamy, checking to stop and stir the milk every 5 seconds. Stir the remaining chopped lavender into the milk, then set aside to cool completely, about 15 minutes.

6. Strain the lavender from the milk and add 1½ tablespoons of the milk to a large bowl. Add the remaining 1 cup confectioners' sugar and whisk until smooth, adding more lavender milk, ½ teaspoon at a time, until a thick but pourable glaze is formed.

7. Working with one shortbread biscuit at a time, use a small offset spatula to spread the glaze on top of the biscuit, then quickly sprinkle or press the edible flowers directly into the glaze. Allow the biscuits to sit for at least 1 hour to set before serving.

GUNTER'S TEA SHOP

Gunter's Tea Shop offers a most charming venue for an amorous rendezvous, where a courting couple may convene with tea and sweet confections. It serves as the backdrop for a scene of notoriety within the annals of Bridgerton history: Simon's single-minded indulgence in his ice cream. This spectacle, without a doubt, prompted Daphne to reevaluate the nature of their relationship, after cooling herself down with a fan.

Gunter's Tea Shop existed in real-life Regency England; it was nestled within the elegant No. 7-8 Berkeley Square, in the heart of London's West End. But the similarities end there. During this period, the tearoom we envision is a mere figment of our imagination. Coffeehouses reigned supreme in this era, and it was quite a social taboo for ladies to grace them with their presence. Gunter's was a confectionery shop and would have offered delights like candied fruits, sweetmeats, jams, sugar-coated nuts, wafers, gingerbread, petite cakes, creams, jellies, and ices crafted into various forms. Of course, one could also procure coffee, tea, and liqueur from the shop's well-stocked shelves. Some of these confectionery shops had small tables or counters where customers could enjoy sweet indulgences, paired with a steaming cup of tea or a glass of wine—an early precursor to the tea rooms of later years.

TRADITIONAL SCONES

———— ❄ ————

Daphne takes particular delight in the afternoon tea break. Scones are a quintessential component of tea, served with jams crafted from berries sourced from the estate and thick Cornish clotted cream. Clotted cream is made by gently heating heavy cream for many hours, until a crust forms on top—with the delightful crust being the most prized part. Outside Britain it can be hard to obtain clotted cream, but a mixture of heavy cream and mascarpone flavored with a little vanilla is equally luxurious.

Makes 10 scones

2 large eggs plus 1 egg yolk

½ cup plus 1 teaspoon milk, plus additional if needed

3 cups all-purpose flour, plus additional for dusting

¼ cup sugar

1 tablespoon plus 2½ teaspoons baking powder

Kosher salt

½ cup (1 stick) unsalted butter, cut into cubes, at room temperature

Clotted cream, for serving

Fruit jam or preserves, for serving

SPECIAL EQUIPMENT:
1 (2½-inch) round biscuit cutter

COOK'S NOTE: *For cheese scones, reduce the sugar to 2 tablespoons and add 1½ cups (about 5 ounces) shredded sharp cheddar cheese (preferably English-style) and 1 teaspoon English mustard powder after the butter has been worked into the flour mixture (and before you add the milk and egg mixture). With the addition of the cheese, this recipe yields 11 scones instead of 10. Best fresh, scones keep for up to 2 days in an airtight container and are best when warmed for a few minutes in a hot oven before serving.*

1. Line a large baking sheet with parchment. In a small bowl, whisk together 2 eggs and ½ cup of the milk until smooth.

2. In a large bowl, whisk together the flour, sugar, baking powder, and 1 teaspoon salt. Sprinkle the softened butter cubes into the flour mixture and use your hands to rub in the butter until the mixture breaks into fine crumbs.

3. Drizzle half the milk and egg mixture over the flour, then gently toss and stir with your hands. Add the remaining milk and egg mixture, then use your hands to gently bring everything together to form a soft and supple dough. (If the dough is a touch dry, stir in additional milk, a tablespoon at a time, to help it come together.)

4. Lightly dust a work surface with flour, then top with the dough. Gently turn the dough over on itself several times until it is smooth, then pat into a round that is

recipe continues

———— ❄ ————

¾ inch thick. Dip a 2½-inch round biscuit
cutter into flour, then use it to cut out 8 scones.
(Do not twist the cutter while cutting, as that
will prevent the scones from rising properly.)
Transfer the scones to the baking sheet, spacing
them about 1 inch apart. Lightly press the dough
scraps together, re-roll, and cut out 2 additional
scones. Chill the scones in the refrigerator for 20
minutes.

5. Preheat the oven to 425°F.

6. Whisk the egg yolk and the remaining
1 teaspoon milk in a small bowl until smooth,
then brush the tops of the scones with the egg
wash. Bake until the scones are puffed and
golden brown, about 15 minutes, rotating the
baking sheet once after 10 minutes. Transfer the
scones to a wire rack and let cool for 10 minutes.
Place the warm scones on a large platter and
serve with clotted cream and fruit jam or
preserves.

THE PERFECT SCONE

Scones originated as griddle cakes before transitioning to
oven-baked treats, during a history that spanned centuries.
A perfect scone should possess enough flavor to stand on
its own merit, yet not overwhelm the cream and jam that's
generously spread on top. When baked to perfection, a
distinctive crack forms in the middle, where the scones rise
during baking. This crack allows you to effortlessly split the
scone, yielding two flawless halves.

THAT ICE CREAM
No-Churn Bourbon-Cherry Ice Cream

———— ❈ ————

Daphne will never forget the sight of Simon savoring a moment with his ice cream during their outing to Gunter's. This bourbon-cherry ice cream earned the Duke's seal of approval, and might just win over the Duchess with its elegance. A sophisticated and boozy ice cream, for adults only, it requires the full attention of its taster.

Makes 6 to 8 servings

1 cup dried sweet cherries, halved	1 (14-ounce) can sweetened condensed milk	2 cups heavy cream, cold
½ cup (4 ounces) bourbon	Kosher salt	½ cup roasted unsalted hazelnuts, coarsely chopped

PRE-FREEZER ICE CREAM

During the Regency era, ice creams were prepared by chilling flavored cream in a heavy pewter canister that was then placed in a wooden bucket filled with ice and salt. A special spatula was used to stir the cream at intervals until it transformed into delicate ice cream. The right amount of salt kept the ice from melting, and the pewter was a perfect material to absorb cold, transferring it to the cream. The method employed here for this ice cream closely mirrors the historical approach, and requires nothing more than a loaf pan, a spatula, a freezer, and a bit of time, showing that you do not absolutely need a large ice cream maker.

1. Place a metal or glass 9 by 5-inch loaf pan in the freezer to chill while you make the ice cream base.

2. In a small bowl, combine the dried cherries and bourbon. The cherries will not be fully submerged, and that is okay. Set aside to plump the cherries, about 2 hours, stirring occasionally. Strain the cherries and reserve the bourbon; you should have about ¼ cup.

3. In a medium bowl, whisk together the condensed milk, the reserved bourbon, and ¼ teaspoon salt.

4. In a large bowl, use an electric hand mixer set on medium speed to whip the cream until stiff peaks form, about 2 minutes. Use a rubber spatula to fold several large spoonfuls of the whipped cream into the condensed milk mixture, then pour it into the bowl with the rest of the whipped cream. Gently fold together until just combined (there should be no streaks of whipped cream). Pour into the chilled loaf pan, cover, and freeze until thick and creamy, like soft-serve ice cream, about 3 hours.

5. Use a spoon to swirl in the bourbon-soaked cherries and chopped hazelnuts. Place the plastic wrap directly on top of the ice cream and continue to freeze until firm, about 6 additional hours.

6. Scoop out the ice cream into serving cups and serve.

———— ❈ ————

TREACLE OLD-FASHIONED

———— ❖ ————

This is a robust drink designed for the Duke and Duchess, crafted by concocting a rich, sticky base with treacle syrup and water, then combining it with bourbon and several dashes of bitters. The concoction is stirred with ice until very cold, then poured over ice cubes and garnished with a twist of orange peel for added fragrance. It's the perfect tipple for Daphne and Simon to savor by the fire on a chilly winter evening.

Makes 1 serving

2 to 3 teaspoons Treacle Syrup (recipe follows)

4 dashes orange bitters

1 large square or round ice cube

¼ cup (2 ounces) premium bourbon

1 (3-inch) strip of orange peel

1 Luxardo maraschino cherry, for garnish (optional)

COOK'S NOTE: *Although not a perfect substitute for black treacle, an equal mix of blackstrap molasses and honey stirred together can be used in its place.*

1. In a lowball or rocks glass, combine the treacle syrup and orange bitters. Add the ice cube, then pour the bourbon over the ice. Use a long bar spoon to stir everything together for 1 minute (this will guarantee the cocktail is nicely chilled).

2. Use your hands to hold the orange peel over the glass, then twist it so that some of its essential oils are released into the drink. Snuggle the peel down into the cocktail, garnish with the maraschino cherry (if using; the Duke prefers his without), and enjoy immediately.

TREACLE SYRUP

Makes about ¾ cup

¼ cup sugar

¼ cup black treacle

½ cup water

1. In a small saucepan over medium-low heat, stir together the sugar, treacle, and water. Cook, stirring occasionally, until the sugar and treacle have blended and the mixture is hot and steamy, about 5 minutes. Remove from the heat and cool completely at room temperature.

2. Transfer the syrup to a glass jar. Use immediately or store in the refrigerator for up to 14 days.

———— ❖ ————

THE MONDRICHES' STEAK
and MUSHROOM PIE

❧

*"Boxing is not for all to enjoy; it requires
a strong stomach and an even stronger jaw."*
—WILL MONDRICH

Will and Alice Mondrich are hurtled into the upper echelons of the ton after their son becomes the next Lord Kent. Will is inspired by the real-life story of Bill Richmond, a former enslaved man who ascended to upper-class English society through his boxing talent. The gentlemen of the ton relished placing bets on boxing matches, and Anthony and Simon formed a bond with their favored prizefighter. Simon would even step into the ring to exchange a few punches with the celebrated boxer, who went on to run a boxing gym and later his own gentlemen's club.

This steak and mushroom pie would find its place on the Mondriches' table on special occasions. During leaner times, some of the traditional beef could be substituted with kidney, or even oysters (which were at one point so cheap they became the food of the poor). This is a modest recipe tailored to two people with humble origins—however, a humble pie can ascend the social ladder and become an elegant dish when you decorate the crust beautifully with any leftover pastry dough. This pie has been a staple of pub dinners for centuries, remaining an integral part of British culinary heritage.

Makes 4 to 6 servings

1 sheet frozen puff pastry, defrosted according to the package directions

2 tablespoons vegetable oil

1½ pounds well-marbled boneless beef chuck, cut into ¾-inch cubes

Kosher salt and freshly ground black pepper

12 ounces fresh cremini mushrooms, sliced ¼ inch thick

1 medium yellow onion, coarsely chopped

1 large carrot, cut into ½-inch pieces

2 small celery stalks, sliced ¼ inch thick

1 cup (8 ounces) dark stout beer

3 tablespoons all-purpose flour

2 teaspoons finely chopped fresh rosemary

2 teaspoons finely chopped fresh thyme

1 dried bay leaf

2 cups mushroom or beef stock

2 teaspoons Worcestershire sauce

1 large egg

COOK'S NOTE: *The pie can be prepared in advance and frozen, and it can also be made using leftover stew, whether meat, fish, or vegetarian.*

recipe continues

1. Unfold the sheet of puff pastry on a cutting board and cut the pastry into strips 1 inch wide and approximately 10 inches long (about 9 strips). Transfer the strips to a baking sheet, laying them down in a single layer. Tear a large piece of parchment and place it on your cutting board. Lay 5 of the pastry strips vertically on the parchment about 1 inch apart. Working with the edge of the strips closest to you, fold the first, third, and fifth strips up by 2 inches, then lay 1 pastry strip across the strips at the folds. Unfold the 3 strips so that they cover the crosswise strip.

2. Now, working with the edge of the strips farthest from you, fold the second and fourth strips down over the crosswise strip. Lay another pastry strip crosswise roughly 1 inch above the first crosswise strip, then unfold those second and fourth strips so they cover the new strip. Repeat these steps, weaving the 2 remaining pastry strips crosswise through the vertical strips to create a lattice design.

3. Turn an 8-inch square baking dish upside down, center it over the pastry strips, then firmly press the dish into the pastry to make an indentation of the dish in the lattice. Use a knife to cut away the excess dough. Repeat, and trim again, if needed. Slide the parchment with the lattice onto a small baking sheet (trim the parchment, if needed) and place in the freezer to chill while you prepare the filling.

4. In a Dutch oven over medium-high heat, warm 1 tablespoon of the vegetable oil until it starts to shimmer. Season the beef liberally with salt and pepper, then add half the cubes to the hot oil. Sear the meat on all sides, turning the cubes so they brown evenly, 6 to 8 minutes. Place the seared cubes in a large bowl and sear the remaining beef, and place in the bowl as well.

5. Add the mushrooms to the Dutch oven and cook, stirring occasionally, until tender and browned in spots, about 15 minutes. Place in the bowl with the beef.

6. Add the remaining tablespoon vegetable oil, then add the onion, season with salt and pepper, and cook, stirring frequently, until lightly browned and tender, about 10 minutes. Add the carrot and celery, season with salt and pepper, and cook, stirring frequently, until starting to become tender, 6 to 8 minutes.

7. Add the browned beef and mushrooms (and any juices in the bowl) to the Dutch oven, then pour in the beer and cook until reduced by about half, 5 to 8 minutes. Sprinkle the flour over the mixture and cook, stirring constantly, for 3 minutes. Stir in the rosemary, thyme, bay leaf, stock, and Worcestershire sauce. Stir to combine and bring to a simmer, 3 to 5 minutes. Reduce the heat to medium, partially cover

with the lid, and simmer, stirring occasionally, until the beef is fork-tender and the cooking liquid has reduced to a thick gravy, 1½ to 2 hours. Season with additional salt and pepper, if needed. Remove and discard the bay leaf. Transfer the mixture to the 8-inch square baking dish.

8. Preheat the oven to 400°F.

9. In a small bowl, lightly whisk the egg with a splash of water. Remove the lattice top from the freezer. Brush the top of the pastry with the egg wash, then carefully lay the pastry on top of the filling. Place the baking pan on a baking sheet.

10. Bake until the puff pastry is puffed and deep golden brown and the filling is bubbling, about 40 minutes, rotating the baking sheet once after 25 minutes. Let the pie rest for 10 minutes before serving.

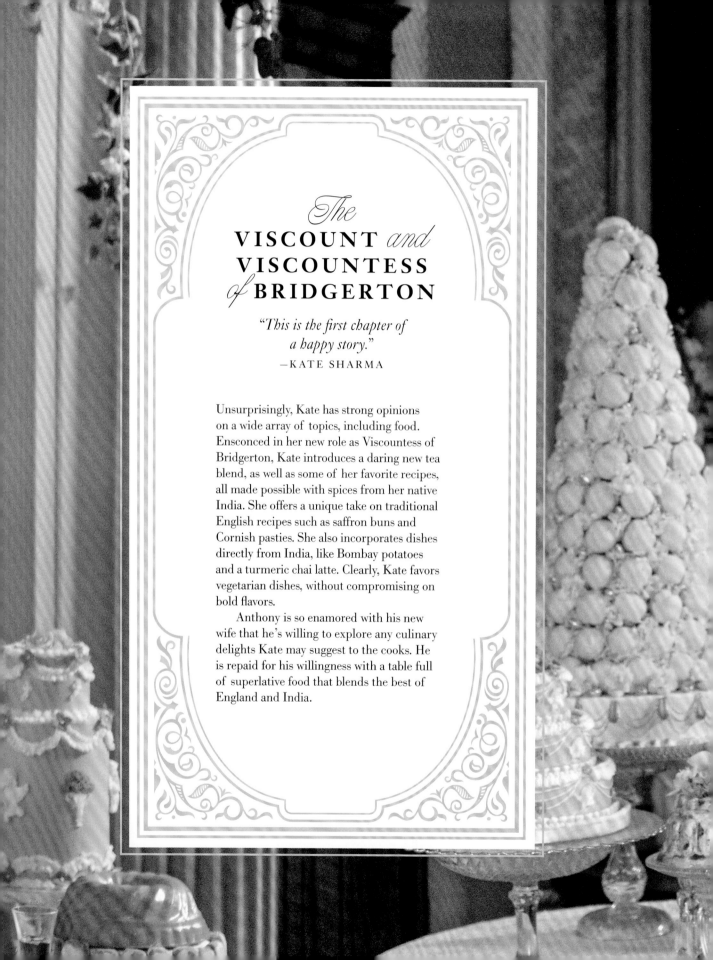

The VISCOUNT *and* VISCOUNTESS *of* BRIDGERTON

*"This is the first chapter of
a happy story."*
—KATE SHARMA

Unsurprisingly, Kate has strong opinions
on a wide array of topics, including food.
Ensconced in her new role as Viscountess of
Bridgerton, Kate introduces a daring new tea
blend, as well as some of her favorite recipes,
all made possible with spices from her native
India. She offers a unique take on traditional
English recipes such as saffron buns and
Cornish pasties. She also incorporates dishes
directly from India, like Bombay potatoes
and a turmeric chai latte. Clearly, Kate favors
vegetarian dishes, without compromising on
bold flavors.

Anthony is so enamored with his new
wife that he's willing to explore any culinary
delights Kate may suggest to the cooks. He
is repaid for his willingness with a table full
of superlative food that blends the best of
England and India.

AKURI ON TOAST

"It is my first week as Viscountess in my new home.
I must make a good impression."
—KATE SHARMA

The Viscountess would have encountered this dish on her trips to Mumbai with her family. Akuri is a preparation of scrambled eggs with onions, tomatoes, chiles, and cilantro and acts as a delicious breakfast, brunch, or even appetizer when served on small toasts.

Makes 4 to 6 servings

8 large eggs

2 tablespoons heavy cream

1½ tablespoons ghee (clarified butter)

½ teaspoon cumin seeds, lightly crushed

½ small red onion, finely chopped

Kosher salt

1 Indian green chile or other medium-hot chile, thinly sliced

1 (1-inch) piece fresh ginger, peeled and finely grated

3 garlic cloves, finely grated

¼ teaspoon ground turmeric

¼ teaspoon mild Indian red chile powder, such as Kashmiri

2 small Roma (plum) tomatoes, finely chopped

2 tablespoons coarsely chopped fresh cilantro, plus whole leaves for garnish

Toasted sliced bread, for serving

1. In a large bowl, combine the eggs and cream and whisk vigorously until pale yellow in color and almost fluffy.

2. In a large nonstick skillet over medium heat, melt the ghee until it starts to bubble lightly. Add the cumin seeds and pan-fry for 30 seconds, stirring constantly. Add the red onion, season with salt, and cook, stirring occasionally, until tender, 6 to 8 minutes. Add the chile, ginger, and garlic and cook for 2 minutes, stirring constantly. Stir in the turmeric and chile powder and cook for 1 minute, stirring constantly. Add the tomatoes and cook, stirring occasionally, until softened, about 5 minutes. Reduce the heat slightly, add the egg mixture, season with salt, and cook, using a heat-resistant rubber spatula to gently stir and scrape as needed, until small, custardy curds form, 8 to 15 minutes. (The timing for this will range greatly depending on the heat of your stovetop.) Remove from the heat and gently fold in the chopped cilantro.

3. Spoon the eggs over slices of toast, top with the cilantro leaves, and serve immediately.

SHARMA CORNISH PASTIES

While traditional Cornish pasties typically have a filling of beef, potato, rutabaga, onion, and a dash of pepper, the Viscountess finds this Indian-inspired filling more appealing, evoking memories of samosas. The filling here contains chickpeas, sweet potatoes, and peas cooked with aromatic Indian spices. When accompanied by a salad, these pasties make an excellent lunch or picnic option, but also can serve as a clever portable meal, perfect for a horseback ride around the Bridgerton estate.

Makes 12 servings

FOR THE DOUGH

1 cup (2 sticks) unsalted butter, cold

2½ cups all-purpose flour, sifted, plus extra for dusting

Kosher salt

1 tablespoon apple cider vinegar

¼ cup ice water

FOR THE FILLING

1¼ pounds large sweet potatoes (about 2), peeled and cut into 1-inch chunks

Kosher salt

¼ cup ghee (clarified butter)

½ cup finely diced yellow onion

2 garlic cloves, minced

2 teaspoons minced fresh ginger

½ teaspoon fennel seeds

½ teaspoon cumin seeds

½ teaspoon ground coriander

¼ teaspoon ground cloves

¼ teaspoon ground cinnamon

¼ teaspoon freshly ground black pepper

½ cup drained and rinsed canned chickpeas

½ cup frozen green peas, defrosted

TO FINISH

1 large egg, lightly beaten

SPECIAL EQUIPMENT:

1 (5½-inch) round biscuit cutter

COOK'S NOTE: *To stock your freezer with pasties, form the pasties and then freeze them on a parchment-lined baking sheet. Transfer the frozen pasties to an airtight container, and freeze for up to 3 months. The pasties can be defrosted and baked according to the recipe's instructions.*

1. MAKE THE DOUGH: In a food processor, add the butter, flour, and 1 teaspoon salt and pulse until the mixture resembles grated parmesan. In a small bowl, stir together the vinegar and ice water. With the food processor running, stream in the water, 1 tablespoon at a time, until the dough comes together into a loose ball. (You may not need all the water; the dough should be moist but not wet.)

2. Spread a large sheet of plastic wrap on a work surface. Turn the dough out onto the plastic and form into a disk that is 1 inch thick. Wrap the dough and chill in the refrigerator until firm, about 2 hours or up to 3 days.

recipe continues

3. MAKE THE FILLING: In a medium saucepan, combine the sweet potatoes and 1 teaspoon salt and cover with cold water. Turn the heat to medium-high, bring the water to a boil, then reduce to a simmer and cook until the potatoes are fork-tender, 10 to 12 minutes. Drain the potatoes, place in a medium bowl, and use a wooden spoon to lightly smash the potatoes to a chunky mash.

4. In a large skillet over medium-low heat, melt the ghee. Add the onion, garlic, ginger, fennel seeds, cumin seeds, coriander, cloves, cinnamon, pepper, and 1 teaspoon salt. Cook, stirring frequently, until the onion is softened, 2 to 3 minutes. Stir in the chickpeas and green peas and cook until warmed through. Add the sweet potatoes, stir to combine, and cook until the sweet potatoes absorb the ghee, 2 to 3 minutes. Transfer the mixture to the same bowl and let cool completely at room temperature, about 1 hour.

5. ASSEMBLE AND BAKE: Place a rack in the center of the oven and preheat the oven to 375°F. Line a baking sheet with parchment.

6. Remove the chilled dough from the refrigerator and let sit at room temperature for 10 minutes, or until the dough can be rolled without cracking. Lightly dust a rolling pin and a work surface with flour. Roll the dough into a disk that is ⅛ inch thick. Use a 5½-inch round biscuit cutter to cut out 6 to 8 rounds. Place the rounds on the baking sheet. Gather the remaining dough into a ball and re-roll, adding more flour as needed. Cut additional rounds until you have 12.

7. Place a dough round on your work surface and add ¼ cup of the cooled filling in the center. Brush the edge of the dough with the beaten egg, then fold the top half over the filling, meeting the bottom edge so you form a half-moon shape. Pinch the edges together to seal the dough and gently push down to remove any air. Crimp the edge between your thumb and index finger or use a fork. Place the pasty on the baking sheet and repeat with the remaining rounds. Brush the tops again with the beaten egg.

8. Bake the pasties until the pastry is golden brown, 45 to 50 minutes, rotating the baking sheet once after 30 minutes. Let the pasties cool for 10 minutes on the baking sheet, then transfer to a platter and serve warm.

FILLETS OF MACKEREL
with Fennel, Gooseberries, and Chile

*"But really the simplest of a Viscountess's tasks is also the hardest one.
Making every person feel as though they are the most important person
in the room. Because most people believe they are."*
—VIOLET BRIDGERTON

This recipe could easily find its place on the menu of a top British restaurant today,
thanks to its fresh and light flavors, complementing a fish that's plentiful in British
waters. The tangy gooseberries offset the fish's richness, and the fennel elegantly ties
the two together with its delicate flavor. Despite its modern appeal, this recipe was
discovered in a Georgian cookbook. The Viscountess loves adding a hint of chile for
an extra burst of color and heat.

Makes 4 servings

¼ cup golden syrup (or honey or agave syrup)

⅓ cup white wine vinegar

3 tablespoons (1½ ounces) dry white wine

4 ounces fresh gooseberries, any blossoms removed, or goldenberries (about ¾ cup; see page 149)

1 small Indian extra-hot red chile pepper, such as a bird's eye, thinly sliced

Dash of freshly grated nutmeg (optional)

Kosher salt and freshly ground black pepper

4 mackerel fillets (4 to 5 ounces each), skin on, pin bones removed

1½ tablespoons vegetable oil

1 teaspoon English mustard

2 teaspoons fresh lemon juice

1 tablespoon extra-virgin olive oil

½ cup very thinly sliced fennel, plus 2 tablespoons hand-torn small frond pieces

¼ cup fresh flat-leaf parsley leaves

1. In a small saucepan over medium heat, warm the syrup, stirring frequently, until
it turns a slightly darker shade of golden brown and starts to smell caramelized,
about 5 minutes. Add the vinegar and wine, increase the heat slightly, and continue
to cook, stirring occasionally, until the sauce is reduced to about ¼ cup (the
consistency will be similar to a thin syrup), about 20 minutes. Add the gooseberries,
chile, nutmeg (if using), and a pinch of salt. Cook, swirling the pan occasionally (do
not stir or you risk crushing the berries), until the berries are just tender but still
hold their shape, about 5 minutes. Remove from the heat and set the mixture aside to
cool; it will thicken as it cools.

recipe continues

2. Use a sharp knife to score the skin on each mackerel fillet several times, then season the fish liberally with salt and pepper. In a large cast-iron skillet over medium-high heat, warm 1 tablespoon of the vegetable oil until it starts to shimmer. Add half the fillets skin side down and cook until the skin is golden brown and crisp, about 3 minutes. Gently press down on the fish so all the skin is in direct contact with the skillet. Gently flip the fish over and cook on the flesh side until the fish is lightly browned and just cooked through, about 1 minute. Transfer the fish to a large plate or baking sheet, add the remaining ½ tablespoon vegetable oil to the skillet, and cook the remaining fillets.

3. In a medium bowl, whisk together the mustard, lemon juice, olive oil, and a large pinch of salt and pepper. Add the sliced fennel, fennel fronds, and parsley, and gently toss to coat in the vinaigrette.

4. Transfer the fish fillets to 4 serving plates, spoon some of the sauce over and around the fish, then place a mound of the fennel salad on top of the fish. Serve immediately.

INDIA PEPPER POT
with Dumplings

While the Sharmas hail from South India, this recipe is inspired by an eighteenth-century recipe for West India pepper pot published in 1788 cookbook *The English Art of Cookery* by Richard Briggs. The book features a few Indian-inspired recipes, demonstrating the taste for Indian flavors among high society in Georgian England. This Indian pepper pot is a lamb curry, showcasing an array of spices without overwhelming the senses—a flawless curry for an opulent feast.

Makes 6 to 8 servings

1½ tablespoons Indian mild red chile powder, such as Kashmiri

2 teaspoons ground turmeric

2 teaspoons paprika

2 teaspoons fenugreek leaves

½ teaspoon ground mace

½ teaspoon ground allspice

¼ teaspoon ground cloves

1½ tablespoons vegetable oil, plus additional for greasing

2 pounds boneless lamb shoulder, cut into 1-inch cubes

Kosher salt

1 large yellow onion, coarsely chopped

2 teaspoons coriander seeds, finely crushed

2 teaspoons cumin seeds, finely crushed

2 large carrots, peeled and cut into ½-inch dice

2 large celery stalks, trimmed and cut into ½-inch dice

1 (1½-inch) piece fresh ginger, finely grated

4 garlic cloves, finely grated

5 cups vegetable stock

4 baby turnips (about 6 ounces total), peeled and cut into ½-inch wedges

1⅓ cups self-rising flour

3 tablespoons thinly sliced scallion greens

¾ cup shredded vegetable suet

3 tablespoons cold water, plus additional as needed

2 cups (lightly packed) coarsely chopped trimmed turnip greens, mustard greens, or kale leaves

Coarsely chopped fresh cilantro, for garnish

COOK'S NOTE: *Vegetable suet (or shortening), made from vegetable oil and hydrogen gas, is used in this recipe because it makes for the fluffiest dumplings (and is Kate's preferred choice), but you can also use standard suet, which is made from beef fat.*

1. In a small bowl, stir together the chile powder, turmeric, paprika, fenugreek, mace, allspice, and cloves.

2. In a Dutch oven over medium-high heat, warm 1 tablespoon of the vegetable oil until it starts to shimmer. Season the lamb liberally with salt, then add half to the hot oil. Sear the meat on all sides, turning the cubes so they brown evenly, 6 to 8 minutes total. Transfer the seared meat to a large plate, add the remaining ½ tablespoon vegetable oil, sear the remaining lamb, and combine with the first batch.

recipe continues

3. Reduce the heat slightly, then add the onion, season with salt, and cook, stirring frequently, until tender, 8 to 10 minutes. Stir in the coriander and cumin seeds and continue to cook, stirring frequently, until the onion is softened and lightly caramelized in spots, 6 to 8 additional minutes. Add the carrots and celery, season with salt, and cook until starting to become tender, 6 to 8 minutes. Add the ginger and garlic and cook, stirring constantly, for 2 minutes. Return the lamb to the pot and sprinkle the spice mix over the meat and vegetables. Stir to combine, then cook, stirring constantly, for 2 minutes.

CURRY

The credit for publishing the first "curry" recipe written in English goes to Georgian cookbook author Hannah Glasse, who included one in her 1747 cookbook. This means that curry, or the English adaptation of Indian cuisine, was already an established dish by that time. Curry was served at the Norris Street Coffee House in London's Haymarket as early as 1733. However, the first purely Indian restaurant was the Hindoostane Coffee House, which opened in 1810 in London's Mayfair area. (A plaque commemorates its location today.) The restaurant was managed by an Indian man who had served in the army of the East India Company. He understood that many East India Company men returning home longed for the flavors of the food they had enjoyed in India, and he saw a market opportunity for his business. The Sharma ladies, however, would not have been allowed to enter these men-only coffeehouses, so the only way they could experience the flavors of their homeland was by teaching the family cook.

4. Add the stock, stir, increase the heat to medium-high, and bring to a low boil, about 10 minutes. Partially cover with the lid and cook for 30 minutes. Remove the lid, stir in the turnips, and continue to cook until the lamb is fork-tender, about 1 additional hour.

5. Meanwhile, in a medium bowl, combine the flour, scallion, vegetable suet, and ¼ teaspoon salt and stir until fine crumbles form. Drizzle the 3 tablespoons cold water over the flour mixture and stir until a firm but moldable dough forms. (If needed, add more water, 1 teaspoon at a time, to help the dough come together.)

6. Scoop heaping tablespoons of the dough onto a small baking sheet (you should have about 16), then lightly grease your hands with a touch more oil and roll each portion into a small ball and place back on the baking sheet. Chill in the refrigerator while the stew cooks.

7. When ready, stir the turnip greens into the stew and nestle the dumplings partly into the stew. Cover with the lid and cook until the dumplings are puffed and cooked through, 15 to 20 minutes.

8. Ladle the stew and dumplings into individual serving bowls, garnish with chopped cilantro, and serve immediately.

CAST-IRON TANDOORI CAULIFLOWER *and* EGGPLANT STEAKS

with Cucumber Raita and Rice

※

"Tonight, hosting together, I see that we will always remain ourselves."
—KATE SHARMA

Just as we see Kate carrying her own tea blend, she has a set of her own favorite spices, which she encourages her kitchen to explore. In this recipe, cauliflower steaks and thick slices of eggplant (aubergine) are marinated in yogurt and a homemade tandoori spice blend. These steaks are accompanied by a refreshing cucumber raita and served with basmati rice, but they also pair nicely with the Bombay Potatoes later in this chapter (page 185). Although this recipe is vegetarian, the spice mix can be applied to chicken.

Makes 4 servings

1 large eggplant (about 1 pound), cut lengthwise into ¾-inch-thick steaks (about 4)

Kosher salt

1 cup plain full-fat yogurt

1 tablespoon fresh lime juice

2 teaspoons paprika

1 teaspoon Indian mild red chile powder, such as Kashmiri

1 teaspoon garam masala

1 teaspoon ground cumin

1 teaspoon ground turmeric

1 teaspoon fenugreek leaves (optional)

1 (1-inch) piece fresh ginger, peeled and finely grated

4 garlic cloves, finely grated

1 large cauliflower (about 3 pounds), trimmed and cut into 4 (¾-inch-thick) steaks (save any extra cauliflower for another use)

½ cup vegetable oil, plus additional as needed

Cooked basmati rice, warm, for serving

Cucumber Raita, for serving (recipe follows)

1. Arrange the eggplant slices in a single layer in a large baking dish and sprinkle on both sides with a light coating of salt. Set aside so the bitter juices are expelled from the eggplant, about 1 hour. Blot and lightly press the eggplant slices with paper towels so each slice is very dry, then stack on a plate. Wipe out the baking dish.

2. In a medium bowl, combine the yogurt, lime juice, paprika, chile powder, garam masala, cumin, turmeric, fenugreek (if using), ginger, and garlic. Place the

recipe continues

※

cauliflower steaks in the same baking dish (they can be stacked slightly), then brush all over with a little more than half of the spiced yogurt mixture. Stack the eggplant on top of the cauliflower and brush with the remaining yogurt mixture. Let marinate in the refrigerator for at least 2 hours and up to overnight.

3. Place a rack on the bottom shelf of the oven and preheat the oven to 450°F.

4. In a large, well-seasoned cast-iron skillet or nonstick skillet set over medium to medium-high heat, warm 2 tablespoons of the vegetable oil. In batches, liberally season both sides of the vegetables with salt, then sear the marinated vegetables in the hot oil until deeply browned on both sides, about 5 minutes per side. For each batch, add 2 tablespoons of oil to the skillet; eggplant absorbs oil. Transfer the seared vegetables to a large rimmed baking sheet (sheet pan) as they come out of the skillet.

5. Transfer the baking sheet to the oven and roast until the vegetables are deeply browned and tender, 15 to 20 minutes. Use a wide, flat spatula to transfer the tandoori vegetables to a large platter and serve alongside basmati rice and Cucumber Raita.

CUCUMBER RAITA
Makes about 1 1/4 cups

1 cup plain full-fat yogurt	¼ to ½ teaspoon Indian mild red chile powder, such as Kashmiri	2 tablespoons coarsely chopped fresh cilantro leaves and soft stems
1 (4 ounce) Persian cucumber, finely chopped (about ¾ cup)	Kosher salt	Chaat masala, for garnish (optional)
½ teaspoon ground cumin		

1. In a medium bowl, whisk the yogurt until smooth, then stir in the cucumber, cumin, chile powder, a large pinch of salt, and the cilantro. Transfer to a serving bowl and garnish with a light sprinkle of chaat masala (if using).

2. Serve immediately or transfer to a storage container with a tight-fitting lid and store in the refrigerator for up to 3 days.

BOMBAY POTATOES

───── ❧ ─────

The Viscount of Bridgerton welcomes his new wife's influence over the dinner repertoire, particularly when it involves adding excitement to otherwise ordinary potatoes. In this recipe, potatoes are fried with onion, garlic, and pungent fresh ginger, and are seasoned with a blend of warming spices, including cumin, garam masala, coriander, turmeric, mustard seeds, curry leaves, and chile powder. Finally, the dish is garnished with fresh cilantro (which is the coriander plant). As with many recipes containing spices, the potatoes become better the second day, making leftovers into a feast.

These potatoes offer many options; they are great on their own with either crusty bread, chapati, or naan, or when paired with the cauliflower and eggplant steaks (see page 179). For a brunch or lunch, the potatoes can be heated up and served with fried or scrambled eggs.

Makes 4 to 6 servings

2 pounds small waxy potatoes, such as Red Bliss or Yukon Gold	12 fresh curry leaves	½ teaspoon ground coriander
Kosher salt	1 Indian medium green chile (or serrano), thinly sliced	1 teaspoon garam masala
1 teaspoon ground turmeric	1 small yellow onion, thinly sliced	¼ to ¾ teaspoon Indian mild red chile powder, such as Kashmiri
3 tablespoons vegetable oil	1 (1-inch) piece fresh ginger, peeled and finely grated	1 tablespoon tomato paste
1 teaspoon brown mustard seeds	3 garlic cloves, finely grated	2 tablespoons coarsely chopped fresh cilantro leaves and soft stems
1 teaspoon cumin seeds		

1. Cut in half any potatoes larger than 1 inch in diameter, then place the potatoes in a large pot. Add enough cold water to cover the potatoes by 1 inch. Turn the heat to medium-high and bring the water to a boil, about 15 minutes. Reduce the heat to medium, then season generously with salt and stir in half the turmeric. Simmer until the potatoes are almost tender (a fork inserted into a potato should be met with a touch of resistance), 5 to 10 additional minutes. Reserve ¾ cup of the cooking liquid, then use a slotted spoon to transfer the cooked potatoes to a bowl or plate.

2. In a large skillet set on medium to medium-high heat, warm the vegetable oil. Once the oil starts to lightly shimmer, add the mustard and cumin seeds. Fry until they begin to crackle, about 30 seconds, stirring constantly. Add the curry leaves and green chile and fry for 30 seconds, stirring constantly. Add the onion, season with

recipe continues

───── ✦ ─────

salt, and cook, stirring frequently, until tender and lightly browned in spots, about 10 minutes.

3. Add the ginger and garlic and cook for 1 minute, stirring constantly. Add the remaining turmeric, the coriander, garam masala, and chile powder and cook for 30 seconds, stirring constantly. Add the tomato paste and cook for 2 minutes, stirring constantly. Stir in ½ cup of the reserved cooking liquid, reduce the heat to medium, and simmer to let the flavors marry, 2 to 3 minutes, adding more cooking liquid if the onions start to become dry (they should be nicely saucy).

4. Add the boiled potatoes to the pot and mix gently. Cook until the potatoes are fork-tender and have soaked up the flavors of the sauce, about 5 minutes. Season with additional salt, if needed. Transfer to a serving platter, garnish with the cilantro, and serve.

SAFFRON *and* MANGO BUNS
with Lime and Jaggery Butter

❧

This traditional Cornish saffron bun delights the Viscountess because of its generous use of saffron and caraway in the dough, evoking the flavors of her homeland. She has adopted the bun for the Bridgerton household, but has instructed her cook to add chopped sweet mangos, preferring their flavor over the more mundane currants, which are so common in British cuisine. The mango enhances the delicate saffron flavor, enriching it with fruity and floral notes. Caraway seed is traditional in these buns, but can be omitted; it brings a great touch of anise and citrus that lifts the fruitiness of the mango. Kate enjoys these buns served with a lime and jaggery butter that turns a humble bun into a feast.

Makes 8 servings

1 scant teaspoon saffron threads

1⅓ cups whole milk, lukewarm

1 tablespoon plus ½ teaspoon active dry yeast

3½ cups bread flour

⅓ cup sugar

Kosher salt

¼ cup (½ stick) unsalted butter, at room temperature, cut into pats

4 ounces candied mango, finely chopped (about ⅔ cup)

2 ounces candied ginger, finely chopped (about ⅓ cup)

1 teaspoon caraway seeds (optional)

1 large egg

Lime and Jaggery Butter, for serving (recipe follows)

COOK'S NOTE: *Jaggery powder is a popular unrefined sugar used throughout Indian cuisine. It is traditionally made from the sap of sugarcane and has an earthy sweetness to it. Although the taste is quite different, light brown sugar can be used as a substitute here, but since it is sweeter than jaggery, start with 2 tablespoons and then add more if needed.*

1. Use your fingers to finely crumble the saffron threads into a small bowl, then pour ⅔ cup of the lukewarm milk over it. (For an even more vibrant golden hue in your buns, crush the saffron in a mortar and pestle.) Set aside to steep.

2. Pour the remaining ⅔ cup milk into a medium bowl and sprinkle the yeast over the milk. Let sit until the yeast is foamy, about 5 minutes.

3. In a large bowl, combine the bread flour, sugar, and ¾ teaspoon salt, then top with the pats of butter. Pour half the yeast mixture over the butter and use your hand to stir everything together until the mixture becomes almost pebbly in appearance. Add the remaining yeast mixture, then add the saffron and milk. Use one hand to hold the bowl down while you use your stronger hand to stir and lightly knead until the mixture comes together to form a mostly smooth but still tacky dough, about

recipe continues

5 minutes. Let the dough rest for 5 minutes; the flour will hydrate slightly during this time and make any additional kneading much easier.

4. Lightly press the dough down to flatten it slightly so it covers the bottom of the bowl, then scatter the candied mango, candied ginger, and caraway seeds (if using) on top. Fold the dough up and over the mango and ginger, and knead in the bowl until incorporated into the dough. Transfer the dough to a work surface and continue to knead until the dough is smooth and elastic, 7 to 10 minutes. Cover the bowl and set aside until the dough has doubled in size, about 1 hour.

5. Line a baking sheet with parchment.

6. Punch down the risen dough, then knead it several times. Form the dough into a ball and use a bench scraper or knife to divide the ball in half. Roll each half into a ball, then quarter each ball to make 8 pieces. Working with one piece of dough at a time (keep the remaining pieces covered with a kitchen towel), cup your hand over the dough and roll it so the sides smooth out and form a little bun. Place it on the baking sheet and repeat with the remaining 7 pieces, spacing the buns evenly apart to allow room to rise.

7. Loosely cover the buns with a kitchen towel and set aside until almost doubled in size and buns are soft and squishy (similar to jumbo marshmallows), 30 minutes to 1 hour.

8. Preheat the oven to 400°F.

9. In a small bowl, lightly whisk the egg with a small splash of water, then brush the risen buns with the egg wash. Bake until the buns are lightly puffed and deep golden brown, 15 to 20 minutes, rotating the baking sheet once at 10 minutes. Let the buns cool on the baking sheet for 5 minutes, then transfer to a wire rack to cool at least 15 additional minutes. Serve while still warm with the Lime and Jaggery Butter.

LIME AND JAGGERY BUTTER

Makes scant 3/4 cup

3 tablespoons jaggery powder (see Cook's Note)	1½ teaspoons finely grated lime zest	½ cup (1 stick) European-style (or regular) salted butter
2 teaspoons fresh lime juice		

In a small bowl, stir together the jaggery and lime juice, using a small rubber spatula or back of a spoon to crush the larger granules of jaggery. (If the mixture isn't smoothing out, set it aside for 10 minutes to give it some time to dissolve, then give it a good stir and smash again; a few small granules are fine.) Add the lime zest and butter, and stir until smooth. The flavored butter is ready to be served immediately, but can be stored in the fridge in an airtight container or wrapped well in plastic wrap for up to 7 days.

The VISCOUNTESS'S CROWN CAKE
with Coconut Frosting and Gingerbread Biscuit Crown

After the shock of Anthony and Edwina's canceled wedding, the Sharmas, Lady Violet and Anthony Bridgerton, and Lady Danbury gather in a morning room for a discussion. Behind Kate, dressed in purple for the occasion, is a cake adorned with a crown-shaped biscuit, with a matching purple ribbon. Could this foreshadow that Kate will one day wear the Viscountess crown?

When Kate assumed her role as lady of the house, she likely found mukhwas to be a more visually enticing option than candied or plain caraway seeds in this seed cake. Mukhwas consists of candy-coated fennel seeds with different-colored coatings, and is commonly consumed in India after dinner to aid digestion. This recipe results in a colorful cake, reminiscent of a modern confetti cake, but with the added caraway flavor. The coconut frosting and gingerbread crown topper complete the cake.

Makes 8 to 12 servings

FOR THE MUKHWAS CAKE

½ cup plus 6 tablespoons (1¾ sticks) unsalted butter, at room temperature, plus additional for greasing

1⅔ cups all-purpose flour

1¾ teaspoons baking powder

¾ cup granulated sugar

Kosher salt

3 large eggs, at room temperature

¼ cup whole milk

3 tablespoons sweet mukhwas (candied fennel seeds)

FOR THE COCONUT FROSTING

1 (13.5-ounce) can unsweetened full-fat coconut milk, chilled in refrigerator overnight

½ cup (1 stick) unsalted butter, at room temperature

Kosher salt

3 to 3½ cups confectioners' sugar

FOR THE TOPPING

1 to 3 Gingerbread Biscuit Crowns (recipe follows)

Finely chopped candied pineapple

1. MAKE THE CAKE: Preheat the oven to 350°F. Generously grease an 8-inch round cake pan, line the bottom with a parchment round, and butter the parchment.

2. In a medium bowl, whisk together the all-purpose flour and baking powder.

3. In a large bowl, use an electric hand mixer set on medium-high speed to beat the butter, granulated sugar, and ¼ teaspoon salt until light and fluffy, about 2 minutes. Reduce the speed to low and beat in the eggs, one at a time, stopping and scraping down the bowl occasionally. Add a heaping tablespoon of the flour mixture along

recipe continues

with the last egg to prevent the batter from curdling. Then add half the flour mixture and blend on low speed until the batter is almost combined (a few streaks of flour is fine). Add the milk and blend until almost combined, then add the remaining flour mixture and blend until smooth. Switch to a rubber spatula and gently fold in the mukhwas. Spoon the batter into the cake pan and smooth the top.

4. Bake until the cake is puffed, light golden brown, and a cake tester or toothpick inserted into the center comes out clean, about 30 minutes, rotating the cake pan once after 20 minutes. Let the cake cool in the pan for 10 minutes, then invert it onto a wire rack, remove the parchment, and cool completely.

5. MAKE THE FROSTING: Remove the coconut milk from the refrigerator and use a can opener to open the can. The coconut milk should have separated into 2 layers—a layer of thick coconut cream on top and thin milky liquid underneath. Use a spoon to carefully scoop out ⅓ cup of the cream and put it in a large bowl (reserve the coconut milk for another use). To the coconut cream add the butter and ¼ teaspoon salt, then use an electric hand mixer set on medium speed to blend the mixture.

6. Reduce the mixer speed to low and gradually beat in 3 cups of the confectioners' sugar until smooth, then increase the speed to medium-high and whip until light and fluffy, about 2 minutes. If the frosting is a little loose (the consistency will depend largely on the thickness of the coconut cream), beat in the remaining ½ cup confectioners' sugar, a heaping spoonful at a time, until the frosting tightens up.

7. ASSEMBLE AND SERVE: Spread the coconut frosting on top of the cooled cake, then arrange 1 to 3 iced Gingerbread Biscuit Crowns on top. (Alternatively, transfer the coconut frosting to a piping bag fitted with a large decorative tip and pipe the frosting on top of the cake.) Sprinkle the frosting with candied pineapple, then slice and serve.

GINGERBREAD BISCUIT CROWNS

Makes 12 biscuits

½ cup (1 stick) unsalted butter

2 tablespoons golden syrup (or honey or agave syrup)

1 tablespoon black treacle or molasses

1 tablespoon water

½ cup (packed) jaggery powder (see Cook's Note, page 187)

1½ teaspoons ground ginger

1 teaspoon ground cinnamon

¼ teaspoon ground cloves

¼ teaspoon freshly ground black pepper (optional)

Kosher salt

1⅔ cups all-purpose flour, plus additional for dusting

½ teaspoon baking soda

2 tablespoons pasteurized egg whites

2 cups confectioners' sugar

1 to 3 teaspoons fresh lime juice

Decorative sprinkles (optional)

SPECIAL EQUIPMENT:
1 (5-inch) crown-shaped cookie cutter and 1 small piping bag fitted with a fine round tip

1. In a small saucepan over medium-low heat, stir together the butter, syrup, treacle, water, and jaggery powder. Gently warm until the jaggery powder is completely dissolved and the mixture is smooth and creamy, 10 to 15 minutes, stirring frequently and using the side of a rubber spatula to smash the larger bits of jaggery. The mixture will seem broken at first, but it will come together as the jaggery melts. Remove from the heat and pass the mixture through a fine-mesh strainer into a small bowl, pushing down on any jaggery bits so they pass through into the sauce below. Add the ginger, cinnamon, cloves, pepper (if using), and ½ teaspoon salt, and whisk until smooth. Let cool until the mixture is warm but no longer hot and the consistency thickens slightly to resemble thick caramel sauce, about 15 minutes.

2. In a large bowl, whisk together the flour and baking soda. Pour the warm syrup over the flour mixture and use a rubber spatula to stir until a crumbly dough forms. Using your hands, mix until the mixture comes together to form a smooth dough. (It will be soft and feel somewhat greasy, but it will set up once it's chilled.) Transfer the dough to a piece of plastic wrap and form it into a rectangle ¾ inch thick. Wrap the dough and chill it in the refrigerator until firm but not rock-hard and it goes from shiny to matte, 30 minutes to 1 hour.

3. Line 2 baking sheets with parchment.

4. On a lightly floured work surface, roll out the dough to a rectangle a touch thicker than ⅛ inch. Dip a 5-inch crown-shaped cookie cutter into a bit of flour, then use to cut out crown-shaped biscuits, re-rolling the trimmings as necessary to get 12 biscuits. Place the biscuits on the baking sheets (6 per tray), then use a dry pastry brush or your fingertips to gently brush off any excess flour. Chill until firm, 30 minutes to 1 hour.

recipe continues

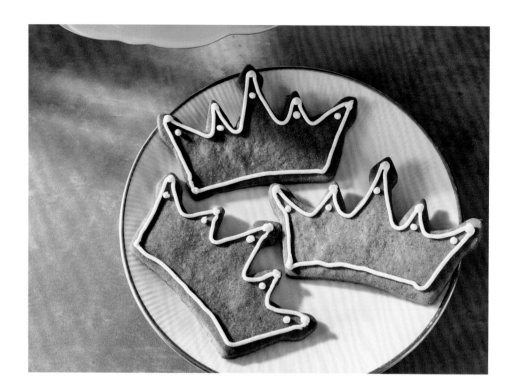

5. Preheat the oven to 350°F. Place the oven rack in the middle of the oven.

6. Bake the chilled biscuits, one tray at a time, until the edges and bottoms are lightly browned, about 15 minutes, rotating the baking sheet once after 10 minutes. Cool the biscuits completely on the baking sheets.

7. In a large bowl, whisk together the egg whites and 2 heaping tablespoons of the confectioners' sugar until smooth. Whisk in 1 teaspoon of the lime juice, then gradually whisk in the remaining confectioners' sugar, a scant ½ cup at a time. (If the icing gets too thick to whisk, switch to a rubber spatula and stir until all the sugar has been added and the mixture is glossy.) The icing will be thick at this point, but stir in additional lime juice, ¼ teaspoon at a time, until it thins to the consistency of toothpaste.

8. Spoon the icing into a small piping bag fitted with a small round tip. Line the edges of the crown biscuits with the icing and decorate with your choice of sprinkles (if using). Set aside until the icing is set, 1 to 6 hours (the time for this depends on the thickness of the icing and the decorations).

GIN COCKTAILS
Two Ways

───── ✦ ─────

Gin, short for genever (or jenever), originated in the region that is now Belgium and the Netherlands, where a Dutch monk distilled juniper berries to create a medicinal remedy with diuretic properties. As is the case with many foods and drinks that have their origins in the medicine cabinet, genever gained popularity as a drink of leisure. By the mid-eighteenth century, there was something of a gin craze in London, and English gin became a preferred alternative to French brandy during the war with France. The Viscount, as a man of principle, would make a point to serve gin instead of brandy to show his allegiance to the English crown.

These two cocktails reflect the personalities of this Bridgerton couple. Anthony, somewhat impatient, prefers a quick cocktail for which everything is prepared in the cocktail shaker. Kate, known for her considerate nature, puts more effort into crafting her drink, using her own spicy syrup created from scratch.

Makes 1 serving each

FOR ANTHONY'S CLASSIC GIMLET

1 tablespoon fresh lime juice

2 teaspoons sugar

2 teaspoons water

¼ cup (2 ounces) gin

Ice cubes

2 small, thin lime wheels, for garnish

FOR KATE'S SPICY GIMLET

2 to 6 whole dried Indian red chiles, such as Kashmiri (mild to medium heat) or bird's eye (extra hot)

¾ cup sugar

¾ cup water

¼ cup (2 ounces) gin

1 tablespoon fresh lime juice

Ice cubes

1 small lime wedge, for garnish

Indian mild red chile powder, such as Kashmiri, for sprinkling

1 MAKE THE CLASSIC GIMLET: In a cocktail shaker, combine the lime juice, sugar, and water. Use a long bar spoon to stir until the sugar is dissolved. Add the gin, fill the shaker with ice, then shake vigorously until chilled.

2 Strain into a coupe cocktail glass, garnish with the lime wheels, and serve immediately.

3 MAKE THE SPICY GIMLET: Use the back of a knife to lightly crush the chiles, then cut away and discard the stems. In a small saucepan over medium heat, combine the

recipe continues

chiles, the sugar, and water and warm gently until the mixture just starts to simmer, about 5 minutes, stirring occasionally. Turn off the heat and set aside until cooled. Allow the chiles to sit in the syrup for an additional 1 to 2 hours, then strain through a fine-mesh strainer into a pint jar or other storage container. Discard the chiles.

4. In a cocktail shaker, combine the gin, lime juice, and 1 tablespoon of the syrup. Fill the shaker with ice, shake vigorously until chilled, then strain into a small rocks glass filled with additional ice cubes. Sprinkle the lime wedge lightly with some chile powder and place it on the side of the glass. Serve immediately.

5. Store the remaining spicy syrup in the refrigerator for up to 14 days.

GOLDEN CHAI

❦

"I despise English tea."
—KATE SHARMA

This turmeric-flavored chai latte is pure Regency luxury, brimming with the Indian flavors that quicken the Viscountess's spirits. Alongside its classic masala spices, the chai incorporates fresh turmeric to infuse the tea with a beautiful golden hue. It's then garnished with frothy milk and served with a whole cinnamon stick—a precious commodity during the Regency era, costing as much as a week's wages if you were part of the working class. The recipe serves two because Anthony nowadays prefers his wife's chai to the dark, bitter coffee served in the coffeehouses of London.

Makes 2 servings

10 whole cloves

12 black peppercorns

6 green cardamom pods

4 cinnamon sticks

2 teaspoons freshly grated peeled turmeric, or 1 teaspoon ground turmeric

1 (1-inch) piece fresh ginger, peeled and sliced into thin rounds

2 tablespoons loose black tea, such as Assam

1½ cups water

1½ cups whole milk, coconut milk, or nondairy milk of choice

2 to 3 tablespoons honey or sugar

COOK'S NOTE: *Alternatively, you can use 2 to 4 black tea bags instead of the loose tea.*

1. In a mortar or shallow bowl, combine the cloves, peppercorns, cardamom pods, and 2 of the cinnamon sticks. Using a pestle, lightly crush the spices, then transfer to a medium saucepan. Add the turmeric, ginger, black tea, and water. Set the heat to medium to medium-high and bring the mixture to a low boil, about 5 minutes. Reduce the heat to medium-low, cover with a lid, and simmer for 5 minutes.

2. Remove the lid, add ¾ cup of the milk and as much honey or sugar as you like, and increase the heat to medium. Warm the tea and milk until the mixture starts to simmer, about 5 minutes, stirring frequently, then continue to simmer for 1 to 2 minutes.

3. Meanwhile, in a small saucepan over medium heat, warm the remaining ¾ cup milk until hot, about 5 minutes. Then tip the hot milk to one side of the saucepan and make it frothy using a milk frother or by whisking it until doubled in size.

4. Using a small fine-mesh strainer, strain the chai into two mugs. Discard the solids. Divide the frothed milk between the 2 mugs and spoon any remaining milk froth on top. Garnish with the remaining cinnamon sticks and serve immediately.

LADY EDWINA'S
SEMIYA PAYASAM

Semiya payasam is a dessert from southern India that resembles rice pudding but is made with vermicelli. The coconut milk brings sweetness and depth of flavor. This is a delicate dessert that evokes the gentle character of Edwina. True to her character, the otherwise plain pudding is transformed by the addition of fragrant green cardamom pods.

Makes 4 to 6 servings

2 tablespoons ghee (clarified butter)

¼ cup raw cashews

¼ cup raw shelled pistachios

⅓ cup golden raisins

1 cup broken semiya (vermicelli)

2¼ cups whole milk, plus additional if needed

1 (13.5-ounce) can unsweetened coconut milk

6 green cardamom pods, lightly cracked

⅓ cup sugar, plus additional to taste

COOK'S NOTE: *If you want to be fancy and add a hint of saffron to your semiya payasam, crumble ¼ to ½ teaspoon of saffron threads into a small bowl and steep with 2 tablespoons warm milk until the milk turns a vibrant golden color. Add to the semiya payasam along with the sugar.*

1. In a large, heavy-bottomed saucepan over medium heat, melt the ghee. Add the cashews and pistachios and cook until lightly browned and toasted, stirring frequently, about 5 minutes. Use a slotted spoon to transfer the nuts to a paper-towel lined plate to drain. Add the raisins to the saucepan and cook until they puff up slightly, stirring frequently, about 1 minute. Place in a small bowl.

2. To the remaining ghee in the saucepan, add the broken semiya and cook over medium heat, stirring frequently, until toasted and lightly golden, about 5 minutes. Add the milk, coconut milk, and cardamom pods, and stir to combine. Bring the mixture to a simmer, stirring and scraping the bottom of the saucepan occasionally, about 20 minutes. At this point, the vermicelli should be tender; if not, continue to cook as needed. (Do not rush this process, since you do not want to scorch the milk mixture.) Add the ⅓ cup sugar and cook for an additional 5 minutes. Turn off the heat and remove the cardamom pods. Taste and stir in additional sugar, if desired.

3. Reserve 1 tablespoon of the raisins and 2 tablespoons of the mixed nuts for a garnish, then stir the remaining into the semiya payasam. It can be served hot, or it can be chilled for serving later. It will thicken as it cools, but you can thin it to your desired consistency by stirring in a splash or two of additional milk.

4. Scoop the semiya payasam into bowls and garnish with raisins and nuts.

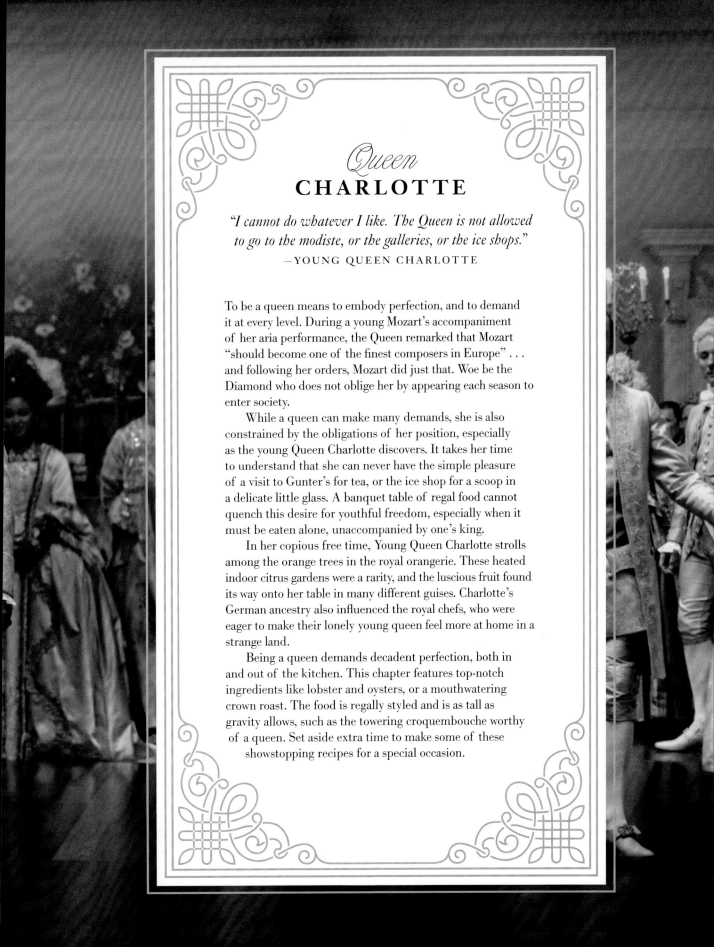

Queen
CHARLOTTE

*"I cannot do whatever I like. The Queen is not allowed
to go to the modiste, or the galleries, or the ice shops."*
—YOUNG QUEEN CHARLOTTE

To be a queen means to embody perfection, and to demand
it at every level. During a young Mozart's accompaniment
of her aria performance, the Queen remarked that Mozart
"should become one of the finest composers in Europe" . . .
and following her orders, Mozart did just that. Woe be the
Diamond who does not oblige her by appearing each season to
enter society.

　　While a queen can make many demands, she is also
constrained by the obligations of her position, especially
as the young Queen Charlotte discovers. It takes her time
to understand that she can never have the simple pleasure
of a visit to Gunter's for tea, or the ice shop for a scoop in
a delicate little glass. A banquet table of regal food cannot
quench this desire for youthful freedom, especially when it
must be eaten alone, unaccompanied by one's king.

　　In her copious free time, Young Queen Charlotte strolls
among the orange trees in the royal orangerie. These heated
indoor citrus gardens were a rarity, and the luscious fruit found
its way onto her table in many different guises. Charlotte's
German ancestry also influenced the royal chefs, who were
eager to make their lonely young queen feel more at home in a
strange land.

　　Being a queen demands decadent perfection, both in
and out of the kitchen. This chapter features top-notch
ingredients like lobster and oysters, or a mouthwatering
crown roast. The food is regally styled and is as tall as
gravity allows, such as the towering croquembouche worthy
of a queen. Set aside extra time to make some of these
showstopping recipes for a special occasion.

POACHED CRAWFISH EXTRAVAGANZA

Towering stacks of crawfish (crayfish) are a common sight on the royal table. Queen Charlotte, reveling in the theatrical, finds greater pleasure when food is artfully stacked to impressive heights. She wishes to be entertained! Historical cookbooks often offer illustrations of dramatic food displays for the cook to mimic, including these seafood towers. If you aren't up for making a tower, try artfully arranging the crawfish and lemons on a generously sized, elegantly vintage serving dish to elevate the dish's visual appeal.

Makes 4 to 6 servings

1½ gallons water

1 cup (8 ounces) dry white wine

1 cup (8 ounces) English dry vermouth

Kosher salt

2 tablespoons black peppercorns

2 tablespoons yellow mustard seeds

6 large sprigs of fresh thyme

3 dried bay leaves

2 shallots, halved lengthwise

1 head of garlic, halved horizontally

4 pounds large live crawfish

⅔ cup mayonnaise

¼ cup whole-grain mustard

2 tablespoons malt vinegar

2 teaspoons Worcestershire sauce

COOK'S NOTE: *If live crawfish are not in season, or not available where you are, you can substitute head-on jumbo shrimp instead. Use kitchen shears to cut through the top of the shells and devein the shrimp (leaving the shells as intact as possible) and cook the shrimp until opaque and just cooked through. The timing should be similar to that for crawfish, but might vary slightly depending on the size and type of shrimp used. Consider saving the crawfish and other seafood shells in the freezer. When a special occasion arises, you merely have to take the shells out of the freezer to make the bisque on page 69.*

1. To a large stockpot on medium-high heat, add the water, white wine, vermouth, ¼ cup salt, the peppercorns, mustard seeds, thyme, bay leaves, shallots, and garlic. Bring to a boil, about 20 minutes, stirring occasionally.

2. Meanwhile, set a large colander in your kitchen sink. Put the crawfish in an extra-large bowl or another large pot. Fill the bowl with cold water and stir several times

recipe continues

to loosen any dirt on the crawfish. Pour the crawfish and the dirty water into the colander and rinse the crawfish under cold running water. Repeat this process several times until the crawfish are clean.

3. Place the cleaned crawfish back into the bowl. Clean the colander and set it back in the sink for later.

4. Add the crawfish to the stockpot and bring back to a simmer, 3 to 5 minutes, stirring occasionally. Continue to simmer until the crawfish turn bright red, about 5 minutes. Drain in the colander and set aside to cool slightly while you make the dipping sauce.

5. In a small bowl, stir together the mayonnaise, mustard, vinegar, and Worcestershire sauce. Season to taste with salt.

6. Use tongs to transfer the warm crawfish to a large platter (leave any aromatics behind, though a few thyme leaves clinging to the shells are fine) and serve with the creamy mustard dipping sauce on the side.

LOBSTER THERMIDOR

Legend has it that lobster Thermidor was initially served to Napoleon Bonaparte. The recipe is said to have been named after the hottest month of the year in the French Republican calendar, falling between July 19 and August 17. An alternate theory suggests it was named after a controversial play (titled *Thermidor*), depicting the French Revolution's culmination, which marked the end of the Reign of Terror. Whichever theory holds true, lobster Thermidor has the rich taste and tantalizing history that make it a perfect fit for Young Queen Charlotte's notion of culinary entertainment.

Makes 4 servings

Kosher salt

2 whole lobsters (about 1½ pounds each)

2 tablespoons unsalted butter

1 small shallot, finely diced

2 garlic cloves, minced

2 tablespoons (1 ounce) cognac

⅔ cup heavy cream

½ teaspoon dry mustard

¼ teaspoon paprika

⅛ teaspoon ground white pepper

Pinch of cayenne

2 large egg yolks, at room temperature

½ cup grated Gruyère cheese

1 teaspoon finely chopped fresh tarragon

COOK'S NOTE: *To save a bit of time, you can purchase cooked lobsters from your favorite seafood monger.*

1. Bring a large pot of salted water to a boil over medium-high heat. While the water is coming to a boil, fill an extra-large bowl with ice water and season it generously with salt.

2. Add the lobsters to the pot of boiling water, cover with a lid, and boil until the shells are bright red, 10 to 12 minutes. Remove the lobsters from the pot and put them directly into the ice water bath.

3. Preheat the oven to 350°F. When cooled, remove the lobsters from the water bath and transfer to a cutting board. Gently twist off the claws, crack the shells, and remove the lobster meat. Transfer the claw meat to a medium bowl. Discard the claw shells (or reserve to make seafood stock). Use a large knife to cut each lobster in half, beginning at the top and cutting along the back all the way down through the tail. Use a small spoon to carefully remove the tail meat and place that in the bowl with the claw meat. Use the spoon to remove and discard the tomalley (and coral, if present; or save coral for another use).

recipe continues

4. Cut the lobster meat into roughly ½-inch pieces, cover the bowl, and chill in the refrigerator while you prepare the shells and sauce.

5. Carefully rinse the lobster halves under cold running water and dry with paper towels. Place the halves on a rimmed baking sheet, cut side down, and roast until dry, about 5 minutes. Turn the halves over and let cool on the baking sheet. Turn off the oven.

6. In a medium saucepan on medium heat, melt the butter. Add the shallot, season with salt, and cook, stirring occasionally, until tender, about 5 minutes. Add the garlic and cook, stirring constantly, until softened, about 1 minute. Stir in the cognac and cook, stirring frequently, until reduced to almost dry, about 2 minutes. Stir in ⅓ cup of the cream, the mustard, paprika, white pepper, cayenne, and a large pinch of salt. Bring to a simmer and cook, stirring occasionally, until the cream mixture is reduced by about half, about 5 minutes. Turn off the heat and cover with a lid.

7. In a small bowl, whisk together the egg yolks and the remaining ⅓ cup cream. Pour into a small saucepan, place on low heat, and simmer, whisking constantly, until the mixture thickens slightly and coats the back of a spoon (it will resemble thin hollandaise sauce), 5 to 8 minutes. Pour the yolk mixture into the saucepan with the cream mixture, then add half the cheese and stir well (it is okay if the cheese doesn't completely melt). Add the lobster and tarragon and stir to combine.

8. Preheat the broiler.

9. Spoon the mixture into the lobster halves and sprinkle evenly with the remaining cheese. Broil the lobsters until the filling is hot and the cheese is golden brown, 4 to 7 minutes.

10. Transfer the stuffed lobster halves to a serving platter and serve immediately.

BROILED OYSTERS
with Herbed Caper Butter

Young Queen Charlotte relishes these savory oysters, as they weren't particularly common in her native Germany. In Regency England, oysters were a treat for the wealthy. Though they were at that time plentiful in the Thames estuary in Kent and Essex, it was no mean feat to transport them to London before they spoiled, which is why they were often pickled. Oysters were eaten in stews and pies, but also on their own as hors d'oeuvres. These oysters harmonize well with the Poached Crawfish Extravaganza (page 204) and the Lobster Thermidor (page 207), creating a seafood extravaganza akin to the sumptuous feasts showcased on the royal table in Bridgerton.

Makes 6 to 8 servings

1 small lemon

½ cup (1 stick) unsalted butter, at room temperature

1½ tablespoons capers in brine, drained well, coarsely chopped

1 large garlic clove, finely grated

1 tablespoon coarsely chopped fresh dill

1 tablespoon coarsely chopped fresh flat-leaf parsley

1 tablespoon sliced fresh chives

Freshly ground black pepper

24 medium or large fresh oysters, such as Rock, Blue Point, or Wellfleet

Rock salt, for serving

1. Finely zest the lemon into a medium bowl. Add the butter, capers, garlic, dill, parsley, chives, and several large grinds of pepper. Stir until well blended.

2. Using an oyster knife, shuck the oysters, twisting the knife to separate the shells and cutting the muscle on the bottom. Reserve the top shells and keep the oysters in their bottom shells.

3. Turn the top shells upside down and arrange them side by side on 2 rimmed baking sheets. Place the bottoms with the oysters in them on top of the shells, adjusting as needed so the shucked oysters sit straight up. Dollop the butter mixture evenly on top of the oysters (about 1 heaping teaspoon each).

4. Preheat the broiler or set the oven to 450°F.

5. One baking sheet at a time, broil or bake until the edges of the oysters begin to curl and the butter is melted, about 5 minutes.

6. Scatter a layer of rock salt on 1 to 2 large serving platters, then nestle the oysters (with the single bottom shell only) in the rock salt. Squeeze a touch of fresh lemon juice on top of each oyster, and serve while still warm.

REGAL ROAST OF LAMB

Shaped like a crown befitting a queen, this aromatic lamb roast draws inspiration
from a recipe originating in the Regency era and a dish served to the Young Queen
at Buckingham House. The transformation of the lamb rack into a crown fittingly
adds a touch of drama.

Makes 4 to 8 servings

2 (1½- to 2-pound) racks of lamb,
large fat cap removed and bones
frenched

Kosher salt and freshly ground
black pepper

2 tablespoons vegetable oil

3 tablespoons chicken or duck fat

2 cups cubed stale country bread

4 ounces white button
mushrooms, finely chopped

1 small yellow onion, finely
chopped

12 ounces (93% lean) ground
chicken

3 garlic cloves, minced

½ cup drained cornichons, finely
diced, and 2 tablespoons brine
reserved

8 large fresh sage leaves, finely
chopped, plus whole sage on the
stem for serving

3 tablespoons coarsely chopped
fresh flat-leaf parsley

½ cup chicken stock

1 tablespoon extra-virgin olive oil

COOK'S NOTE: *The stuffing recipe yields about 4 cups. If your crown roast is on the smaller side, spoon
any extra stuffing into a small baking dish and bake alongside the lamb until hot, 15 to 20 minutes. Cover with
aluminum foil to keep it warm, then serve with the crown roast.*

*If you want to enjoy this same dish, but do not want to make an entire crown roast, you can cut the stuffing
recipe in half and bake it in a small baking dish, then serve it alongside pan-roasted bone-in lamb chops.*

*The stuffing can be made with any ground meat you prefer. Turkey can be used in place of the chicken or, for an
even richer filling, substitute ground pork and use lard or bacon fat in place of the poultry fat.*

1. Place the racks fat side up on a cutting board. Use a sharp knife to cut crosshatch
marks into the fat. Turn the racks bone side up and cut slits 1 inch long and ½ inch
deep between the bones into the thick of the meat. Cut one long slit (about ¼ inch
deep) right at the base of the bones on each rack. Use your hands to bend each rack
to form a semi-circle, then lay out flat again. Season the lamb all over liberally with
salt and pepper.

2. In a large cast-iron skillet on medium-high heat, warm 1 tablespoon of the
vegetable oil until shimmering. Place one rack fat side down in the hot oil and sear
until the fat is lightly browned, 2 to 3 minutes. Transfer the rack to a large baking

recipe continues

sheet. Repeat with the remaining tablespoon of oil and other rack of lamb. Let cool for 5 minutes (reserve the fat in the skillet).

3. To create the crown, lay the racks side by side with the bones facing upward. Use kitchen twine to tie the 2 bones that meet when the racks are pressed together. Sit the racks up on edge, then bend them so their ends meet and form a crown; the bones should be on the outside of the roast. Use twine to tie the 2 bones that meet on the other ends of the racks. Cut an extra-long piece of twine (it will need to tie around the racks 2 or 3 times), then slip the twine into the slit that you cut right at the base and tie it around the roast 2 to 3 times, then secure it with a tight knot. Cut another long piece of twine and tie the top of the bones together so they form a concave shape. Place the crown roast on a rimmed baking sheet and chill in the refrigerator while you prepare the stuffing.

4. To the cast-iron skillet with the leftover lamb fat, add 1 tablespoon of the chicken fat and turn the heat to medium. Scatter the bread cubes in the skillet, season with salt and pepper, and toast, stirring frequently, until golden brown and crisp, 6 to 8 minutes. Transfer to a medium bowl.

5. Increase the heat under the skillet slightly, add 1 tablespoon chicken fat and the mushrooms and cook, stirring occasionally, until deeply browned and caramelized in spots, about 10 minutes. Place the mushrooms in the bowl with the bread.

6. Add ½ tablespoon chicken fat and the onion to the skillet, season with salt and pepper, and cook, stirring occasionally, until tender and lightly caramelized, about 10 minutes. Place the onion in the bowl with the bread and mushrooms.

7. Increase the heat under the skillet to medium-high and add the remaining ½ tablespoon chicken fat. Add the ground chicken, season with salt and pepper, and cook, stirring occasionally and breaking up the meat into crumbles, until cooked through and browned in spots, about 5 minutes. Add the garlic and cook, stirring constantly, until softened, about 1 minute. Pour the cornichon pickling brine over the chicken and cook, stirring frequently, until it has been absorbed into the meat, about 1 minute. Remove the skillet from the heat and stir in the chopped sage. Add the bread cubes, mushrooms, and onions along with the cornichons and parsley. Stir until well combined. Pour the chicken stock over the stuffing and stir again. Taste the stuffing and season with more salt and pepper, if needed.

8. Preheat the oven to 400°F.

9. Brush the crown roast inside and out with the olive oil, then spoon the stuffing into the center, using the back of the spoon to help pack it down. Roast in the oven until an instant-read thermometer inserted into the meaty side of the roast registers

135°F for medium doneness, 30 to 40 minutes, rotating the baking sheet once after 20 minutes.

10. Set a wire rack on a baking sheet. Remove the roast from the oven and use a wide, flat spatula (or two) to lift the roast onto the rack. Cover loosely with aluminum foil and let the meat rest for 15 minutes.

11. Transfer the roast to a serving platter. Cut away the long kitchen twine at the top of the bones (keep the shorter ones on the 2 ends and the longer one around the meat), place the stems of sage around the roast, and serve.

NOTE: *Since the center of the roast is filled with a loose stuffing, it is best to present the roast whole, then take it back into the kitchen to remove the rest of the kitchen twine and cut it into individual chops. Lay the chops on the serving platter and spoon the stuffing on top of the chops, then serve.*

ROASTED RAINBOW CARROTS
with Crumbled Bacon, Walnuts, and Caraway

───── ❧ ─────

Rainbow carrots feel modern, but during the Regency era multicolored carrots were common. When glazed with bacon fat, these colorful carrots are a great side dish. They glisten beautifully, while the walnuts add earthy notes, the bacon contributes savory flavor, and the caraway seeds evoke the Young Queen's German heritage. *Kümmel*, or caraway seeds, are commonly used in Germany in bread, as well as added to meat and vegetable dishes; they bring a nutty taste with hints of anise and citrus.

Makes 4 to 6 servings

1 teaspoon caraway seeds

3 slices bacon, halved crosswise

Grapeseed oil, if needed

⅓ cup unroasted walnut halves

Kosher salt and freshly ground black pepper

1½ pounds small rainbow carrots, peeled, stems trimmed to 1 inch

2 tablespoons coarsely chopped fresh flat-leaf parsley

COOK'S NOTE: *Vegetarians can eliminate the bacon and substitute 3 tablespoons of extra-virgin olive oil for the bacon fat.*

1. Place a rimmed baking sheet on the lowest rack of the oven and preheat the oven to 425°F. In a mortar and pestle, lightly crush the caraway seeds.

2. Arrange the bacon halves in a large skillet in a single layer, then turn the heat to medium. Cook the bacon, turning occasionally, until the fat has rendered and the bacon is crisp, about 20 minutes. Transfer to the paper towel–lined plate to drain any excess fat.

3. There should be about 3 tablespoons of bacon fat remaining in the skillet; remove any additional from the skillet, but if there is not enough, add a small splash of grapeseed oil to reach that amount. Add the walnuts, season lightly with salt and pepper, and toast the nuts in the bacon fat until lightly browned in spots, stirring occasionally, 6 to 8 minutes. Use a slotted spoon to transfer the walnuts to the same plate as the bacon.

4. Turn off the heat and add the carrots to the skillet. Season with salt, pepper, and the caraway seeds, and toss to coat. Remove the hot baking sheet from the oven and carefully add the carrots, spreading them out in a single layer. Place back into the oven and roast the carrots until tender and golden brown in spots, about 20 minutes, turning the carrots once after 15 minutes.

5. Chop the toasted walnuts, then transfer to a small bowl along with the parsley. Crumble the bacon and stir into the walnuts and parsley. Transfer the roasted carrots to a serving platter, top with the crumbled bacon and walnuts, and serve.

───── ❧ ─────

ROYAL ASPARAGUS
with Horseradish Hollandaise Sauce

In Germany, white asparagus, known as *spargel,* are preferred to green asparagus. White asparagus are the same plant as green, but they are cultivated by blanching, depriving them of light during growth and thereby preventing them from acquiring the green color. For the German-born Queen Charlotte, asparagus would have been exclusively white—imagine her delight at seeing asparagus gracing her plate in a beautiful shade of green. But whether green or white, Hollandaise is a preferred sauce for asparagus. In this recipe, the addition of horseradish imparts a hint of heat. Traditionally, asparagus with Hollandaise is served with the smallest boiled new potatoes available.

Makes 4 to 6 servings

2 pounds medium asparagus, tough ends trimmed	½ cup (1 stick) unsalted butter, melted	Kosher salt and freshly ground black pepper
3 large egg yolks	1 tablespoon prepared horseradish, drained if needed	Sliced fresh chives, for garnish
2 teaspoons fresh lemon juice		

1. Fill a large pot with 1 inch of water and set in a steamer insert or basket. Bring the water to a boil over medium-high heat, then lay the asparagus in the steamer (some overlap is fine, or you can do this in 2 batches depending on the size of your pot and steamer). Cover and steam until the asparagus is crisp-tender, 2 to 3 minutes. Cover and keep warm.

2. Fill a medium saucepan with 1 inch of water and bring to a simmer over medium-high heat. In a large stainless-steel or heatproof glass bowl that fits snugly over the saucepan, combine the egg yolks and lemon juice and vigorously whisk until thickened and doubled in volume. Reduce the heat under the saucepan so the water maintains a slow simmer, then place the bowl over the saucepan. Slowly drizzle in the melted butter while whisking constantly and rapidly until the mixture becomes paler in color and has thickened to the consistency of thick heavy cream, scraping down the sides of the bowl occasionally with a rubber spatula, if needed. (It is important to cook the Hollandaise on moderate heat so the egg yolks do not scramble.) Remove the sauce from the heat, whisk in the horseradish, and season to taste with salt and pepper.

3. Transfer the asparagus to a platter, then drizzle half the warm sauce over. (If the sauce has gotten too thick, whisk in a few drops of warm water to loosen it.) Garnish the dish with the chives and serve immediately, with the remaining sauce on the side.

CHARLOTTE ROYALE

The Charlotte Royale stands out as a beloved showstopper on the Bridgerton royal table. The original "Charlotte" is said to have been created in honor of the historical Queen Charlotte. The earliest English recipe for it dates back to 1808, and was featured in Maria Rundell's cookbook, *New System of Domestic Cookery*. That initial version consists of slices of the finest white bread enveloping an apple compote. That's because during the Regency era in Britain, fine white bread held a prestige similar to that of cake. Subsequent variations of the recipe feature Bavarian cream and ladyfingers replacing the bread, and were referred to as a Charlotte Russe. In the twentieth century, the Charlotte Royale emerged, substituting the ladyfingers with slices of a pretty Swiss roll.

Makes 10 to 12 servings

FOR THE CAKES

Unsalted butter, for greasing

4 large eggs

2 large egg whites

¾ cup granulated sugar

1 tablespoon vanilla extract

Kosher salt

1½ cups cake flour, sifted

1 cup blackberry jam

3 cups fresh blackberries

Confectioners' sugar, to serve (optional)

FOR THE FILLING

5 teaspoons unflavored powdered gelatin

1¾ cups cold whole milk

¾ cup granulated sugar

1 teaspoon vanilla extract

2 (3.1-ounce) bars ruby chocolate, coarsely chopped

¾ cup heavy cream

1½ cups crème fraîche

COOK'S NOTE: *While the cake and filling fit perfectly into a 3-quart bowl with a diameter of 8½ inches at the top, you could use a slightly larger bowl. The most important factor is that you measure the bowl's diameter from one inner edge to the opposite inner edge, then choose a round cake pan that is about ½ inch smaller than that diameter. This way, the round cake layer will fit perfectly on the bottom of the dessert no matter the size of the bowl you use. Ruby chocolate is a pink-hued chocolate with a slightly tart and fruity taste; if ruby chocolate is unavailable, white chocolate can be substituted in the filling. The recipe for the Swiss roll can also be used in the recipe for Trifle on page 88.*

1. MAKE THE CAKES: Lightly grease the bottoms of an 8-inch round cake pan and a 13 by 18-inch rimmed baking sheet (half-size rimmed baking sheet or sheet pan), then line both bottoms with parchment. (Do not grease the parchment.)

2. Preheat the oven to 350°F.

recipe continues

3. In a large bowl, combine the eggs, egg whites, granulated sugar, vanilla, and ¼ teaspoon salt. Use an electric hand mixer on high speed to whip the mixture until it doubles in size and becomes pale yellow and fluffy, 5 to 7 minutes.

4. With the mixer turned off, add the cake flour to the egg mixture in 3 batches, using a rubber spatula to fold the flour into the batter after each addition. (It is important to make sure all the flour in a batch is incorporated before adding more.) Pour enough batter to come up the sides of the round cake pan by ½ inch. Pour the remaining batter into the baking sheet. Use an offset spatula to spread the batter to the edges of both pans and smooth the tops. Bake both cakes until a toothpick inserted into the center of each cake comes out clean (the cakes should remain pale yellow and not start to brown), 15 to 17 minutes. It is especially important to bake the sheet cake until just done; if that cake overbakes, it will break when rolled.

5. Remove the cakes from the oven and let cool just enough to be handled. Carefully flip the round cake over and out of the cake pan onto a flat plate, then remove the parchment and cool completely. Wrap the cooled cake with plastic and refrigerate.

6. Working quickly while the sheet cake is still warm, gently lift it out of the baking sheet using the edge of the parchment and carefully pull it onto a cutting board. Spoon the blackberry jam on top, spreading it evenly from edge to edge. Turn the cake so the long sides are parallel to your countertop. Lift the parchment on the bottom of the cake away from the edge of the cake and gently roll up the cake forward into a tight log, pulling away the parchment with every roll so it doesn't get caught up in the cake. Cover the roll with plastic wrap and refrigerate until completely cooled, about 1 hour.

7. MAKE THE FILLING: Put the gelatin in a large bowl. Pour ½ cup of the milk over the gelatin and stir to combine. Set aside for the gelatin to bloom, about 5 minutes.

8. To a medium saucepan on medium heat, bring the remaining 1¼ cups milk, the granulated sugar, and vanilla to a simmer, whisking occasionally to dissolve the sugar, about 5 minutes. Pour the hot milk over the gelatin and whisk until the gelatin is completely dissolved. Add the chopped chocolate and whisk until melted. Let cool to room temperature; do not let the mixture get cold or the gelatin will start to set.

9. In another large bowl, combine the cream and crème fraîche. Use an electric hand mixer fitted with the whisk attachment and set on high speed to whip until stiff peaks form, about 3 minutes. Fold the whipped cream into the cooled chocolate mixture in 3 batches, making sure each addition is completely incorporated before folding in more cream. The filling should have a creamy smooth texture.

10. ASSEMBLE THE DESSERT: Line with plastic wrap a 3-quart metal or glass bowl that is approximately 8½ inches in diameter. More than one sheet of plastic wrap can be used; just make sure it is pressed firmly against the inside of the bowl.

11. Remove the cake roll from the refrigerator and take off the plastic wrap. Use a serrated knife to cut the roll into ½-inch rounds, wiping the knife often to make clean cuts, about 24 slices. Place one cake slice on the bottom of the bowl in the center. Arrange the slices against the side of the bowl, working in a circle around the first piece and pressing them snuggly against each other. Make sure the swirls of the roll all go in the same direction and don't worry if there are small gaps between the slices—these will be filled in later. Continue to add the slices until the entire bowl is lined. Also, don't worry if a little cake extends above the edge of the bowl—this will be pressed down later.

12. Using about a third of the blackberries, press the tip of a blackberry gently into any spaces between the cake slices. Pour a third of the filling into the cake-lined bowl, then add half the remaining blackberries, spreading them evenly over the filling. Add another third of the filling, then scatter the remaining blackberries on top. Spread the remaining filling over the top of the blackberries.

13. Remove the cake layer from the refrigerator, unwrap it, and place it on top of the filling; it should fit neatly within the top edge of the bowl (this tight fit will ensure an even bottom when the dessert is flipped). Press the cake layer gently into the filling, then cover the bowl with plastic wrap. Place a plate on top of the bowl to help press down and gently compress the dessert. Refrigerate for at least 12 hours and up to overnight to give the filling ample time to set.

14. SERVE: Remove the plastic wrap on top and invert the cake onto a serving plate, guiding it with the plastic wrap on the bottom of the bowl. Gently remove the bowl and discard the plastic wrap. Dust the top with confectioners' sugar (if using). Use a serrated knife to slice the cake into thick wedges and serve. (Store any leftover cake, covered in plastic wrap, in the refrigerator for up to 3 days.)

JAUNE MANGE

"Brimsley, I will get my own oranges from now on."
—QUEEN CHARLOTTE

This sunny jelly draws its inspiration from a recipe dating back to 1773, and it is infused with the citrusy scent of the orangerie Young Queen Charlotte so adores. This rendition features the regal kumquat, the queen of citrus. Despite their petite size, kumquats boast an immense flavor, though let's be honest—one would only squeeze a kumquat for a queen!

Jaune mange, which translates to "yellow food," is a cousin of another historical upper-class jelly known as blanc mange, or "white food." In a truly regal manner, this jelly was typically crafted in a mold shaped like the sun, although any suitable mold or large bowl will suffice. Moreover, this jelly can be equally delightful when prepared in smaller molds or served in dainty glasses.

Makes 4 servings

Vegetable oil, for greasing

1 pound kumquats, halved

3 tablespoons sugar

Kosher salt

¾ cup (6 ounces) semi-sweet white wine, such as Riesling

3 tablespoons cold water

1 tablespoon unflavored powdered gelatin (1 envelope)

3 large egg yolks

SPECIAL EQUIPMENT:
4 (½-cup) jelly molds or ramekins

COOK'S NOTE: *You can also make the Jaune Mange in a 2-cup jelly mold but allow at least 8 hours for it to set; it might take even longer depending on the depth of the mold.*

1. Lightly dip a folded paper towel into the vegetable oil, then wipe 4 (½-cup) jelly molds or ramekins with the oil, making sure to get into the crevices if your molds have an intricate design. Place the greased molds on a small baking sheet.

2. Squeeze the juice from the kumquats into a medium bowl (it is okay if seeds fall into the juice), then drop the kumquat halves into the bowl as well. Add the sugar and a small pinch of salt and stir to combine. Set aside for 30 minutes, stirring occasionally. During this time, the sugar and salt will help coax the essential oils out of the skins of the kumquats.

recipe continues

3. Strain the mixture through a fine-mesh strainer set over another medium bowl, pressing down firmly to extract as much syrupy juice as possible. Measure the kumquat syrup; you should have ½ cup. If you have less, add water to make up the difference. Set the kumquat syrup aside, and save the bowl and strainer setup.

4. In a medium saucepan over medium heat, warm the wine until hot and steaming, about 2 minutes. Remove from the heat.

5. Place the cold water in a small bowl, then sprinkle the gelatin over. Let sit for 1 minute for the gelatin to bloom, then stir it into the warm wine until the gelatin dissolves.

6. In a large bowl, whisk the egg yolks until smooth. Gradually whisk the wine mixture into the egg yolks, then whisk in the kumquat syrup. Pour the mixture through the strainer into the bowl, then discard the kumquat solids.

7. Skim off any foam that forms on top of the liquid. Divide the mixture among the molds, then cover and chill in the refrigerator until completely set, at least 6 hours and up to overnight.

8. When you are ready to unmold, wet one of your hands and use it to loosen the jelly in one of the molds or ramekins. Allow the jelly to slide out onto a lightly wet plate; the wet plate allows you to easily move the jelly around if necessary. Repeat to unmold the remaining three jellies, then serve.

QUEEN'S CAKES

One of the earliest recipes for these aptly named Queen's Cakes appeared in Robert Smith's cookbook, *Court Cookery,* in 1725. These cakes are considered the ancestors of cupcakes, and they are traditionally made with equal proportions of flour, butter, eggs, and currants. We reduced the currants by half and the sugar by a bit in this recipe to match the Queen's preference for lighter cakes. The Queen's Cakes are then flavored with orange flower water and a touch of precious mace. All these ingredients were expensive during the Georgian period and indicate that this recipe was beyond the means of ordinary people.

During the Regency era, specialized tins were created specifically for baking these delicate little cakes. You can bake them in any small baking dishes you have or in a muffin tin. Baking powder was not invented until the mid-nineteenth century, so the Regency Queen's cakes would have been denser. If you'd like to taste them as Queen Charlotte would have, you can simply omit the baking powder. However, once baking powder was invented, it quickly became a staple used in nearly every cake recipe.

Makes 12 servings

Nonstick cooking spray

1 cup all-purpose flour

1½ teaspoons baking powder

10 tablespoons (1¼ sticks) unsalted butter, at room temperature

⅔ cup granulated sugar

¼ teaspoon mace (optional)

Kosher salt

2 large eggs, at room temperature

1 tablespoon orange blossom water

½ cup dried currants

1 tablespoon raw or turbinado sugar

COOK'S NOTE: *Alternatively, you can leave the tin ungreased and use cupcake liners, or use 12 small individual baking tins (preferably nonstick), making sure to grease your tins well.*

1. Spray the cups of a 12-cup muffin tin with nonstick spray.

2. In a medium bowl, whisk together the flour and baking powder.

3. In a large bowl, use an electric hand mixer set on medium-high speed to beat together the butter, granulated sugar, mace (if using), and ¼ teaspoon salt until light and fluffy, about 3 minutes. Reduce the speed to low and beat in the eggs, one at a time, stopping and scraping down the bowl occasionally. Beat in the orange blossom water and add 1 tablespoon of the flour mixture (this will keep the batter from

recipe continues

curdling). Then add the remaining flour mixture and use a rubber spatula to stir until the batter is just combined and smooth. Do not overmix. Fold in the currants.

4. Cover the batter with plastic wrap and set aside to rest for 30 minutes at room temperature. The batter will become somewhat fluffy during this time and the currents will plump up slightly. This will help ensure a light crumb—but not too light, since Queen's Cakes are known for being slightly dense.

5. After 20 minutes, preheat the oven to 350°F.

6. Divide the batter among the cups in the muffin tin (about a scant ¼ cup per muffin). Do not flatten the batter; leave it in fluffy mounds. Sprinkle the tops with the raw sugar.

7. Bake until the cakes are puffed, the tops and edges are light golden brown, and a cake tester or toothpick inserted into a center cake comes out clean, about 20 minutes, rotating the muffin tin once after 15 minutes. Cool the cakes in the muffin tin for 5 minutes, then flip over to remove from the tin and place on a wire rack to cool completely before serving. Store any leftover cakes in an airtight container at room temperature for up to 5 days.

CHARLOTTE'S PINK PERFECTION

Raspberry Cream Macaron Sandwiches

When you are queen, you can request food to match your attire. These delightful large pink macaron sandwich cakes, filled with raspberry buttercream and fresh raspberries, might appear on Queen Charlotte's table when she dons her pink dress. This quixotic coordination elicits a smile on a day otherwise weighted with the task of hosting audiences at the palace. Fortunately, among those visitors is frequently Queen Charlotte's dear friend and confidante, Lady Danbury, who takes great pleasure in jesting about the opulent spread always laid out in Her Majesty's honor.

Macarons were not a part of the Regency period's food culture, but in the Bridgerton universe they have become a fixture because of their colorful appearance and versatility. A biscuit called "macaroon" did indeed exist in the real Regency era, but it resembled more of what we would now refer to as an amaretti biscuit—slightly more rustic and dense, certainly not delicately sandwiched with a delightful filling.

Makes 10 large sandwiches

FOR THE MACARONS

2 cups confectioners' sugar, sifted

2 cups superfine almond flour, sifted

6 large egg whites

Kosher salt

1 cup granulated sugar

6 drops pink gel food coloring, plus additional as needed

FOR THE RASPBERRY BUTTERCREAM

3¾ cups fresh raspberries

1 cup (1 stick) unsalted butter, at room temperature

6½ cups confectioners' sugar, sifted, plus more as needed

Kosher salt

2 teaspoons vanilla extract

Edible gold flakes, for garnish (optional)

SPECIAL EQUIPMENT:

1 large piping bag fitted with a ½-inch straight pastry tip and another with a ½-inch star tip

1. MAKE THE MACARONS: Line 2 baking sheets with parchment. In a medium bowl, whisk together the confectioners' sugar and almond flour.

2. In the bowl of a stand mixer fitted with the whisk attachment, whip the egg whites and ¼ teaspoon salt on medium speed until frothy, 1 to 2 minutes. Add the granulated sugar and the food coloring and continue to whip until medium peaks

recipe continues

form, 8 to 10 minutes. (If you want a more vibrant shade of pink, fold in another drop or two of food coloring.)

3. Remove the bowl from the mixer and use a rubber spatula to fold in half the almond flour and confectioners' sugar until just combined. Add the remaining almond flour and confectioners' sugar and fold until fully combined. Continue to fold until the batter is smooth, shiny, and slowly flows from the spatula when you lift it above the bowl. This is called *macaronage*. This can mean folding the batter for several minutes, but be patient and do not stop until you reach macaronage. If you are unsure, test the batter by dolloping a small amount onto a plate; if the batter is ready, it will hold its shape and any ridges will gently smooth out.

4. Transfer the batter to a large piping bag fitted with a ½-inch straight pastry tip. Keeping the bag in a vertical position, pipe the batter into 3½-inch circles on the baking sheets, about 10 per sheet. When piping the macarons, keep the tip in the center of the circle, gently squeezing the bag and allowing the batter to spread out on its own into a circle. Leave about 2 inches of space between the macarons, as the batter will spread slightly while baking. Tap the baking sheets lightly on the counter 3 or 4 times to allow air bubbles to rise to the top. Use a toothpick or cake tester to pop any bubbles, which will ensure a smooth macaron top.

5. Leave the macarons out at room temperature until they form a skin on top, are no longer sticky to the touch, and the color becomes matte and slightly paler, about 1 hour. (The timing for this will depend on the humidity of your environment.) Do not rush this process or the macarons will crack as they bake.

6. Place racks in the upper third and lower thirds of the oven and preheat the oven to 300°F.

7. Bake the macarons until they puff slightly, are set completely, and no longer shift at their base when you gently touch the tops, about 30 minutes. Let cool completely on the baking sheets, set atop wire racks.

8. MAKE THE BUTTERCREAM: Put 1¼ cups of the raspberries in a blender and blend until very smooth. Set a fine-mesh strainer over a small bowl, then pour the raspberry puree through the strainer. Discard the seeds.

9. In the bowl of a stand mixer fitted with the paddle attachment, combine the butter, confectioners' sugar, and ¼ teaspoon salt. Mix on medium speed until smooth and creamy, about 3 minutes. Scrape down the sides of the bowl, add the raspberry puree and the vanilla and mix on medium-high speed until smooth, creamy, and fluffy, 2 to 3 minutes. The buttercream should hold a stiff peak; if it is too loose, add more confectioners' sugar, ¼ cup at a time, until you reach the desired consistency. Transfer to a large piping bag fitted with a ½-inch star tip.

10. ASSEMBLE THE DESSERT: Use a small offset spatula to gently remove the macaron shells from the baking sheets. Lay 10 macaron shells, bottom sides up, on a clean work surface. Pipe the buttercream in a circular motion, starting from the outside of the shells and leaving a ¼-inch border around the edges (similar to the top of a cupcake with a peak in the center).

11. Press some of the remaining raspberries into the edges of the buttercream, arranging them side by side so they cover the entire macaron. Place the remaining 10 macaron shells on top of the buttercream, then gently press down to adhere the top shell to the buttercream.

12. Lightly sprinkle the edible gold onto the tops and edges (if using). Serve at room temperature or refrigerate, lightly covered with plastic wrap, for up to 3 days. The macarons can be served straight from the refrigerator or you can leave them out for about 30 minutes to let the filling warm slightly before serving.

CROQUEMBOUCHE

Queen Charlotte delights in being dazzled by the most exquisite culinary creations, and so Her Majesty holds a deep affection for this towering confection, which can rival the height of her elaborate coiffure. *Croquembouche* is French for "crack in the mouth," and these traditional choux puffs (cream puffs) are topped with a brittle layer of caramel for decoration. This caramel layer bonds the tower of choux together and cracks when you take a bite. The choux puffs are brimming with a pastry cream infused with the delicate essence of tea, adorned with a craquelin topping that looks pretty but also imparts additional structure to the choux. In French, this intricate confection is called a *pièce montée* ("mounted piece") and is exclusively prepared for weddings and special occasions.

Makes 12 to 16 servings

FOR THE CRAQUELIN TOPPING

½ cup (1 stick) unsalted butter, at room temperature

½ cup plus 1 tablespoon (lightly packed) light brown sugar

1 cup all-purpose flour, sifted

FOR THE CHOUX PASTRY

1 cup water

½ cup whole milk

¾ cup (1½ sticks) unsalted butter, cut into small cubes

1 tablespoon granulated sugar

Kosher salt

1½ cups all-purpose flour, sifted

4 large eggs

FOR THE TEA PASTRY CREAM

3 cups whole milk

3 tea bags of choice, such as Earl Grey, English Breakfast, jasmine, or white tea

Ice cubes

6 large egg yolks

⅔ cup granulated sugar

¼ cup cornstarch

Kosher salt

3 tablespoons unsalted butter, cut into small cubes

FOR THE CARAMEL

½ cup water

2 cups granulated sugar

Edible flowers, for garnish (optional)

SPECIAL EQUIPMENT:
1 (12-inch tall) Styrofoam cone with a 4- to 4½-inch base; 1 (1½-inch) round biscuit cutter; 1 piping bag fitted with a ½-inch straight pastry tip

COOK'S NOTE: *Any flavor of tea will work and be delicious in this pastry cream, but the tea you choose will affect the color of the finished cream. For a light yellow pastry cream, use a floral jasmine or white tea. For a darker pastry cream, use a robust black tea such as Earl Grey or English Breakfast.*

1 MAKE THE TOPPING: In the bowl of a stand mixer fitted with the paddle attachment, cream together the butter and brown sugar on medium-high speed until lightened in color and fluffy, 2 to 3 minutes. Scrape down the sides of the bowl, add

recipe continues

the flour, and mix on medium speed until the mixture just comes together and looks similar to cookie dough, about 1 minute.

2. Transfer the dough to a piece of parchment and top with a second piece of parchment. Roll the dough out until it is ⅛ inch thick. The thickness is important, but not the dimensions of the dough as long as it stays between the parchment sheets. Refrigerate the dough until chilled, about 20 minutes.

3. Line a baking sheet with parchment.

4. Use a 1½-inch round biscuit cutter to cut the dough into as many disks as possible. Use an offset spatula to transfer the disks to the baking sheet. Re-roll the dough and continue cutting disks until you have 80. (If at any point the dough becomes too warm to roll, place it back in the refrigerator to chill and then continue the cutting process.) Chill the disks in the refrigerator while you make the choux pastry.

5. MAKE THE PASTRY: In a medium saucepan over medium-high heat, stir together the water, milk, butter, granulated sugar, and ¼ teaspoon salt and bring to a boil, about 5 minutes. Turn off the heat, add the flour, and use a wooden spoon to stir it into the wet ingredients until a dough is formed. Reduce the heat to medium and cook, stirring constantly, until there is a thin film at the bottom of the saucepan, about 3 minutes.

6. Transfer the dough to the bowl of a stand mixer fitted with the paddle attachment. Mix on medium speed until the dough is slightly cooled, 3 to 4 minutes, scraping down the sides of the bowl as needed. When the dough is warm but not super hot, mix in the eggs, adding one at a time and mixing well between additions. Continue to mix until the dough is smooth and glossy, 1 to 2 minutes. Transfer the dough to a piping bag fitted with a ½-inch straight pastry tip. (The choux pastry can be made ahead and stored in the refrigerator until you are ready to pipe and bake the following day.)

7. Place a rack in the upper third and a rack in the lower third of the oven and preheat the oven to 375°F. Cut 2 pieces of parchment to line 2 baking sheets, but do not use to line the sheets yet.

8. Pipe a small amount of choux pastry into the 4 corners of each baking sheet, then lay the parchment on the baking sheets and press down on the corners; this will ensure the parchment doesn't lift up while you pipe out the dough.

9. Pipe the choux pastry into mounds on the baking sheets that are 1 inch wide and 1 inch tall, leaving 1½ inches of space between them; you should have about 40 mounds per baking sheet.

CROQUEMBOUCHE

Although mentions of the croquembouche appeared a few years before he published his book *Le Pâtissier Royal Parisien* in 1815, the French pastry chef Antoine Carême is credited with inventing this breathtaking choux tower. In 1816, Carême, considered the first celebrity chef, accepted the position of head chef to George IV, Prince Regent. It is therefore possible that Carême prepared the croquembouche for Queen Charlotte, even though he stayed on as chef to the Prince Regent only briefly in his career.

10. Use a small offset spatula to transfer the craquelin disks onto the tops of the dough mounds. Arrange the disks so they sit flat in the center of the mounds, then lightly press down to adhere the disks to the dough.

11. Bake until the pastries have puffed and the craquelin disks have baked into the tops and become golden brown (they will almost melt into the pastry as it bakes and create a craggy topping), about 30 minutes. Remove from the oven and use a skewer to poke a hole in the bottom of each puff; this will help release steam. Transfer the puffs to a wire rack to cool completely.

12. MAKE THE PASTRY CREAM: In a large saucepan set on medium to medium-high heat, combine the milk and tea bags and bring to a simmer, stirring frequently to prevent the milk from scorching, about 5 minutes. Remove from the heat and let the tea steep for 15 minutes. Place a fine-mesh strainer over a medium bowl. Fill a large bowl halfway with ice cubes and cold water (ice bath).

13. In the bowl of a stand mixer fitted with the whisk attachment, combine the egg yolks, granulated sugar, cornstarch, and ¼ teaspoon salt and whip on high speed until doubled in size and pale yellow in color, about 2 minutes.

14. Remove the tea bags from the hot milk and discard. With the mixer on low speed, gradually add the steeped milk to the egg yolk mixture. (Do not rush this process or you will scramble the eggs.) Pour the mixture back into the saucepan and cook over medium-low heat, constantly whisking gently, until the mixture thickens to the consistency of pudding and you begin to see bubbles reach the surface, about

recipe continues

3 minutes. Turn the heat off and stir in the butter, 2 or 3 cubes at a time, until melted and the pastry cream is smooth and glossy. Strain the pastry cream through the fine-mesh strainer to remove any lumps, then place the bowl of pastry cream into the ice bath and stir until completely cooled. Transfer the pastry cream to a piping bag fitted with a small, straight tip and store in the refrigerator until ready to use.

15. MAKE THE CARAMEL AND ASSEMBLE THE DESSERT: Wrap a 12-inch Styrofoam cone (see Special Equipment, earlier) with parchment or foil and use tape to hold it in place. (Alternatively, make a cone out of flexible poster board to approximate these dimensions.) Place the cone on a serving platter or cake board.

16. Pipe the pastry cream into the bottom of each puff where you had poked the hole; the pastry cream should fill the puffs.

17. When all the puffs are filled, make the caramel. Carefully pour the water into a medium saucepan without splashing the sides of the pan (otherwise, this will cause crystallization). Gently sprinkle the granulated sugar over the water, again being careful not to splash the water. Turn the heat to medium and cook, without stirring, until the sugar turns amber in color (similar to honey), 10 to 12 minutes. If you have a candy thermometer, the temperature should register about 295°F. Remove the saucepan from the heat.

18. Working quickly but very carefully, dip the side of a cream puff into the caramel, then place it at the bottom of the cone; the first puff will act as a base as you build the croquembouche upward. Now, dip the right or left side of a second puff into the hot caramel and press the caramel side to the first puff. Continue to dip the sides of the puffs in the hot caramel and arrange the puffs side by side, working your way up the cone until you reach the top (this method adheres the puffs to each other and not to the cone.) It is important to work quickly and carefully while the caramel is hot.

NOTE: *If you are working in a cool and dry space, and would like to remove the cone, do that now by gently lifting the croquembouche off the cone and placing it back on the serving plate. However, it is not necessary to remove the cone; to guarantee the structure of the croquembouche, no matter your environment, it is recommended you leave it on the cone and move on to the next step.*

19. As you work with the hot caramel, you will notice the residual heat turn it from amber to a darker hue, similar to maple syrup. At this point the sugar will form thin threads when you dip a metal fork into it and lift it up. Pull those threads of sugar around the cone to create a web of spun sugar. (If the caramel becomes too stiff to work with, place it over low heat and gently reheat until the sugar creates the threads again.)

20. With the croquembouche covered with spun sugar, and sitting securely on the serving platter, you can add your decorative edible flowers (if using) and serve.

PISTACHE POUR DEUX

———✦———

BRIMSLEY: *We would serve them together.*

REYNOLDS: *A lifetime?*

BRIMSLEY: *Yeah. A lifetime.*

REYNOLDS: *Great love can make miracles.*

Picture Reynolds searching the kitchen at Kew Palace to procure a special treat, in anticipation of Brimsley's arrival with the Young Queen Charlotte. Considering that pistachios were meant only for the tables of the rich, this dish would be a perfect luxurious treat for Reynolds and Brimsley to savor during an impromptu romantic tryst.

Makes 6 servings (4 for guests and 2 for Brimsley and Reynolds)

¾ cup milk	2 teaspoons cornstarch	1 tablespoon orange blossom honey
1¼ cups heavy cream	Kosher salt	Good-quality extra-virgin olive oil, for drizzling (optional)
Ice cubes	6 ounces raw shelled pistachios (about 1½ cups)	
5 large egg yolks, at room temperature	3 cups water	Coarsely chopped toasted unsalted pistachios, for garnish
⅓ cup sugar		

1. In a heavy-bottomed medium saucepan, combine the milk and ¾ cup of the cream. (Chill the remaining ½ cup cream so it is easier to whip later.) Bring the milk mixture to a simmer over medium heat, stirring occasionally, about 5 minutes. Cover and keep warm. Place a fine-mesh strainer over a medium bowl. Fill a large bowl halfway with ice cubes and water (ice bath).

2. In a medium bowl, whisk the egg yolks and sugar together until creamy and slightly thickened, 1 to 2 minutes. Whisk in the cornstarch and a small pinch of salt. Slowly and gradually whisk the hot milk mixture to the yolk mixture, then pour back into the saucepan. Turn the heat to medium and whisk constantly until the custard thickens and leaves a path on the back of a spoon when a finger is drawn across it, 5 to 7 minutes. (The consistency will be similar to a thin pudding.) Spoon the custard into the strainer and use the back of a spoon to press it through to the bowl below. Place the bowl in the ice bath and stir until the custard is cooled down. Cover with a piece of plastic wrap directly on top of the custard and chill until completely set, at least 2 hours and up to overnight.

recipe continues

———✦———

3. Put the raw pistachios into a medium bowl. Pour the water into a small saucepan and bring to a boil over medium-high heat, about 5 minutes, then pour the hot water over the pistachios and allow to sit for 3 minutes. Drain the pistachios and rinse under cold water until completely chilled.

4. Scatter the nuts on a clean kitchen towel. Allow to sit for 5 minutes, then fold the towel over the nuts and rub back and forth several times to release the skins as much as possible. Shake loose and discard the skins, then pick through with your fingers to remove any remaining skins. This will help ensure a bright green pistachio paste.

5. Place the pistachios in a food processor and blend until the nuts break down into fine moist crumbles, about 5 minutes. Turn off the food processor for 5 full minutes. (This allows the food processor to cool down slightly.) After 5 minutes, continue to blend the pistachios until a smooth paste forms, about 5 additional minutes. Again, turn off the food processor for 5 minutes, then blend until the paste starts to separate and green pistachio oil starts to seep out, about 3 additional minutes. (This green oil will help ensure the pistachio cream is a nice green.) Add the honey, blend for 1 minute, then add the chilled custard and blend until smooth. Spoon the pistachio custard back into the same bowl and cover; chill in the refrigerator while you whip the cream.

6. In a medium bowl, whip the remaining ½ cup cream until stiff peaks form, then fold into the pistachio custard. To serve, spoon the pistachio cream into 6 small serving glasses, drizzle with extra-virgin olive oil (if using), and garnish with toasted unsalted pistachios.

VIN D'ORANGERIE

Made with Mixed Citrus

In the Regency era, oranges were like precious jewels, grown only in the orangeries of the royal palace. This refreshing recipe ensured not a single orange would ever go to waste. This wine offers a blend of tartness, sweetness, and a touch of bitterness because of the blend of citrus used. It's easy to prepare, even if you don't have a large kitchen, as the Queen does. The only challenge lies in exercising restraint and in refraining from opening the bottle too soon! This wine is equally delightful at room temperature or when served chilled over ice.

Makes 8 (1-cup) servings

1 pound bitter and tart citrus fruits, such as Seville oranges, ruby red grapefruits, and/or kumquats

1 pound sweet oranges, such as navel, Cara Cara, and/or blood oranges

1 large lemon

½ vanilla bean, split, with seeds scraped (optional)

1 cup sugar

2 (750ml) bottles dry white or rosé wine

1¼ cups (10 ounces) vodka

1. Cut the citrus fruits, oranges, and lemon into 8 wedges each, then place in a large 4-quart airtight container with a lid. If using ruby red grapefruit, cut into 12 large chunks and if using kumquats, cut in half. Add the vanilla bean and seeds (if using) and the sugar and give the mixture a good stir. Set aside, stirring occasionally, until the sugar is dissolved and has formed a thick syrup, about 30 minutes. Add the wine and vodka, stir to combine, then cover with the lid.

2. Store the wine in the refrigerator for at least 30 and up to 40 days, giving it a good stir every 3 to 4 days. After this period is up, place a large fine-mesh strainer over a large bowl. Wet several layers of cheesecloth and drape them over the strainer. Strain the wine through the cheesecloth and into the bowl. (The vin d'orange might be a touch cloudy, but the intense flavor more than makes up for that.)

3. Pour the wine into large 1-quart bottles or canning jars, top with lids, stoppers, or T-corks and store in the refrigerator until you are ready to serve. The wine is ready to be enjoyed at this point, but if you have the time and the patience, it tastes even better if it is left to age for several more months, preferably in the refrigerator.

4. Serve the vin d'orange as is, in petite wineglasses, nicely chilled over ice, or use as a mixer to add a slightly bitter (but also sweet) note to a fun cocktail.

RELAXATION TEA
with Toasted Fennel Honey

———— ❧ ————

Running an entire nation can be stressful. This tea, made from fresh flowers and sweet herbs, is perfect for a moment of royal "me time," late at night, after Brimsley brings Queen Charlotte her tea and he retires himself. Chamomile settles the nerves, fennel is an antioxidant and has antiviral effects, while mint and ginger soothe indigestion and lemon balm reduces stress and anxiety to promote sleep. Honey brings sweetness but is also a natural antibacterial, so it can help prevent or fight off infection.

Makes 4 cups

1 tablespoon fennel seeds

½ cup raw honey

4 cups water

Scant ¼ cup fresh chamomile flowers

8 large fresh mint leaves

8 large fresh lemon balm leaves

1 (½-inch) piece fresh ginger, peeled and thinly sliced

Orange and/or lemon wedges, for serving

COOK'S NOTE: *Transfer any leftover fennel honey to an airtight container and store at room temperature for up to 1 year.*

1. In a small saucepan over medium-low heat, gently toast the fennel seeds, stirring frequently, until very fragrant, 3 to 4 minutes. Add the honey and warm it with the fennel seeds, stirring frequently, about 3 minutes (the honey will become runny and fluid when warmed). Turn off the heat and set aside to infuse for 30 minutes, then strain through a fine-mesh strainer to remove the fennel seeds.

2. Pour the water into a medium saucepan and bring to a boil over medium-high heat, about 5 minutes. Remove from the heat and let the water sit for 3 minutes, then add the chamomile blossoms, mint leaves, lemon balm leaves, and ginger; steep for 5 minutes.

3. Strain the hot tea directly into a teapot. To serve, pour the tea into your favorite mugs or teacups, and offer with the fennel honey and orange/or lemon wedges on the side.

SUGGESTED MENUS

A
BRIDGERTON BREAKFAST

Soft-Boiled Eggs *64*
British Sausage Rolls *102*
Tattie Scones *20*

A
LADIES' LUNCH

Madame Delacroix's Melon *94*
Esteemed Ladies Salad *109*
Chilled English Garden
Pea Soup *101*
The Viscountess's Crown Cake *191*
Apple and Thyme Tea Punch *54*

The
PERFECT TEA

Lavender Petticoat Tails *153*
Traditional Scones *155*
Battenberg Cake *85*
Golden Chai *198*

A
ROMANTIC SUPPER

Crab Bisque *69*
Artichokes for Two *140*
That Ice Cream *158*
True Love Biscuits *74*
Vin d'Orangerie *245*

A
DINNER TO IMPRESS

Broiled Oysters *210*
Salmagundi *58*
Regal Roast of Lamb *213*
Cast-Iron Tandoori Cauliflower
and Eggplant Steaks *179*
A Grand Trifle *88*
A Discreet Punch *93*

A
HOLIDAY CELEBRATION

Lobster Thermidor *207*
Impressive Game Pie *129*
Royal Asparagus *219*
Roasted Rainbow Carrots *216*
The Hastings' Christmas Cake *143*

A
SELECT SOIREE

British Sausage Rolls *102*
Devils on Horseback *98*
Pâte de Fruits *105*
Treacle Old-Fashioned *161*

ACKNOWLEDGMENTS

I want to thank Su, our fantastic recipe developer, for her brilliant ideas and for infusing my historical recipes with a delightful dash of *Bridgerton* spice, resulting in a splendid collection of flavorful and vibrant recipes. We dedicated several hours, despite the constraints of differing time zones, to discuss all things *Bridgerton* and to imagine the culinary delights beloved by the characters. We had fun, we got hungry, and we hope everyone who reads this book will feel the fun we had and get hungry to get cooking.

I wish to thank everyone who made this book possible, especially our publisher at Random House, Sarah Malarkey, for this opportunity and for bringing Su and I together. Big thanks to Shonda Rhimes for graciously welcoming us into the *Bridgerton* family. It's wonderful to see how much thoughtfulness Shondaland puts into this amazing series. Thank you for creating this fantastic world and for being so hands-on with this book. Finally, thanks to my husband for understanding that while I was writing a book, I disappear into my words and forget just about anything else. He brings me food while I write about food and forget to eat.

—REGULA YSEWIJN

Thank you, Regula Ysewijn, for joining me on this *Bridgerton* journey and for kindly keeping me in check when my ideas got too wild. You are an amazing force in the food-media world and I feel so lucky we were brought together for this project.

As always, immense gratitude to Sarah Malarkey, Lydia Estrada, and everyone at Random House Worlds for bringing me on to another whimsical cookbook where I get to play with food as my job. Thank you to the extraordinary team at Shondaland for your continued guidance in ensuring we create recipes that every *Bridgerton* fan will love.

I truly could not have completed this cookbook without the expert help of Santos Loo and Ali Clarke, who took on the task of bringing to life eleven of the most epic recipes within these pages. Thank you for being my teammates during the development process and for enlivening the *Bridgerton* universe with your culinary greatness.

Last but not least, hugs and finger hearts to my purple-hued ARMY family for being the best taste testers I could ask for (APOBANGPO).

—SUSAN VU

INDEX

Published in the United States by RANDOM HOUSE WORLDS, an imprint of Random House, a division of PENGUIN RANDOM HOUSE LLC, New York.

Random House is a registered trademark, and RANDOM HOUSE WORLDS and colophon are trademarks of PENGUIN RANDOM HOUSE LLC.

LIBRARY OF CONGRESS CATALOGING-IN-PUBLICATION DATA

Names: Ysewijn, Regula, author. | Vu, Susan, author.
Title: Bridgerton: the official cookbook / Regula Ysewijn with recipes by Susan Vu.
Description: First edition. | New York: Random House Worlds, [2024] | Includes index.
Identifiers: LCCN 2024005104 (print) | LCCN 2024005105 (ebook) | ISBN 9780593725573 (hardback) | ISBN 9780593725580 (ebk)
Subjects: LCSH: Cooking, English. | Bridgerton (Television program) | LCGFT: Cookbooks.
Classification: LCC TX717 .Y73 2024 (print) | LCC TX717 (ebook) | DDC 641.5942—dc23 /eng/20240207
LC record available at https://lccn.loc.gov /2024005104
LC ebook record available at https://lccn.loc.gov /2024005105

Printed in China
on acid-free paper

Unit photography courtesy NETFLIX/ LIAM DANIEL

Editor: SARAH MALARKEY
Production editor: KELLY CHIAN
Editorial assistant: LYDIA ESTRADA
Art director and designer: JENNY DAVIS
Photography: ERIN KUNKEL
Photo assistant: VANESSA SOLIS
Food stylist: NICOLE TWOHY
Food styling assistant: HUXLEY McCORKLE, with JESSIE BOOM, CARRIE BEYER, and ALLISON FELLION
Prop stylist: JILLIAN KNOX
Prop stylist assistant: MARINA FREYTES
Production manager: ANGELA McNALLY
Copy editor: CAROLE BERGLIE
Proofreaders: SASHA TROPP, MELANIE GOLD, ERICA ROSE, MEGHA JAIN
Indexer: GINA GUILINGER

Design element credits for borders and frames:
MRS_KATO/SHUTTERSTOCK.COM
EXTEZY/SHUTTERSTOCK.COM
DN BR/SHUTTERSTOCK.COM

9 8 7 6 5 4 3 2 1

First Edition

ABOUT THE AUTHORS

REGULA YSEWIJN is an internationally acclaimed, award-winning food writer, photographer, and author of six books about food culture, including *The British Baking Book* and *The Official Downton Abbey Christmas Cookbook*. Ysewijn is also a judge of the Belgian version of *The Great British Bake Off* television show. Born in Flanders, the Dutch-speaking region of Belgium, she now lives in Antwerp, Belgium, where she houses her immense library of historical cookbooks.

SUSAN VU lives in a multiverse where she splits her time among Seattle, New York, and wherever her next adventure is. She works as a recipe developer, food stylist, and culinary producer in between chasing her favorite band around the world.

RANDOM HOUSE WORLDS
RANDOMHOUSEBOOKS.COM
COVER PHOTOGRAPHS: ERIN KUNKLE
COVER DESIGN: JENNY DAVIS